Richard Rodgers

488 MADISON AVENUE • NEW YORK 22, N. Y.

Telephone MUrray Hill 8-3640

March
19th
1962

Dearest Diahann,

I have just received your note and I hurry

to tell you how touched I am by it. You

have been one of the happiest and most

gratifying experiences I have ever had

in the theatre. I'm proud of you and deeply

grateful for everything you have done for

me personally and professionally.

Love,

Miss Diahann Carroll
277 West End Avenue
New York 23, New York

The

LEGS are THE LAST

to GO

The LEGS are THE LAST to GO

AGING, ACTING, MARRYING, AND OTHER THINGS I LEARNED THE HARD WAY

Diahann Carroll

with Bob Morris

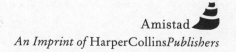

Amistad

An Imprint of HarperCollins*Publishers*

HarperCollins books may be purchased for educational, business, or sales promotional use. For information please write: Special Markets Department, HarperCollins Publishers, 10 East 53rd Street, New York, NY 10022.

FIRST EDITION

Designed by Reshma Chattaram

Library of Congress Cataloging-in-Publication Data has been applied for.

ISBN 978-0-06-076326-8

08 09 10 11 12 WBC / RRD 10 9 8 7 6 5 4 3 2 1

To my friend Josephine Premice-Fales. She was my mentor from the beginning. She was there for the entire experience, supportive and loving through it all. Thank you, my friend.

Contents

The
LEGS are THE LAST
to GO

PROLOGUE

Stepping Out, Senior Style

IT WAS A CLEAR SPRING EVENING IN NEW YORK NOT long ago, and I looked absolutely divine. I felt divine, too, as I stepped out of my hotel onto Central Park South. I was in town from my home in Los Angeles, and had just made an appearance on a talk show with my dear old friend Harry Belafonte. Now I was on my way to a screening at the Tribeca Film Festival. I was feeling incredibly pleased with myself. My new coat—black Armani cut to fit perfectly. And I felt good in it. Well, in New York, your coat is your car, after all, so you have to have one that's just right for all the coming and going.

Although now a Californian, I associate Manhattan with the best of everything. Saks Fifth Avenue, the Metropolitan Museum of Art, and Bergdorf Goodman were around the corner from my hotel. Le Cirque's latest incarnation, a resplendent and colorful room, was east of there. And just a stone's throw from me was the steadfast, palatial Plaza, where I had lived with Suzanne, my only child, in the early 1960s. I performed there in the Persian Room, with a fourteen-piece orchestra. You see, long before I became television's first black actress with her own sitcom, I was a performer in the musical theater and nightclub worlds, with my spiritual center on the stages of Broadway and in the high-end club venues of Manhattan, the Waldorf-Astoria, for example.

Less than a hundred blocks to the north of my hotel stood the brownstone where I grew up, a child of hardworking Harlem parents who made me feel like a princess, even as they struggled to make ends meet. By middle age, I'd soared as far as a girl could possibly soar in a lifetime. I'd surpassed anything anyone in my life could have imagined. Born Carol Diann Johnson, I was a proud graduate of the High School of Music and Art who went on to break more than a few race barriers in her time and more than a few sound barriers while racing around the globe.

Here's the short list: After appearing on Arthur Godfrey's radio show while still in high school, I ended up singing at the Latin Quarter by the time I was eighteen and everywhere else from the Catskills to Las Vegas. At nineteen, I was in my first movie, *Carmen Jones,* with Pearl Bailey and Dorothy Dandridge. Not long after that I was the young lady lip-synching "Summertime" in the movie version of *Porgy and Bess.* That's where I first met Sidney Poitier and started a treacherous nine-year affair. I destroyed my first and most important marriage to Monte Kay, the father of my only child. Other movie roles followed at a young age, including one in *Hurry Sundown* with Jane Fonda, Faye Dunaway, and Michael Caine, and then *Paris Blues,* with Paul Newman, Sidney Poitier, and Joanne Woodward. On

Broadway, as early as 1954, Truman Capote and Harold Arlen had cast me as the ingenue in their Broadway show, *House of Flowers*. And in 1962, Richard Rodgers wrote a musical for me called *No Strings,* in which I played a fashion model in the first interracial romance Broadway had ever seen. That got me a Tony. But there was to be more. In 1968, the networks summoned, and I became NBC's *Julia,* the first sitcom about a black character. I had my own television variety show a few years later. It was called, what else? *The Diahann Carroll Show.* I appeared in every television special imaginable during the years when such things existed, including one in which Sammy Davis Jr. and I sang together in a tribute to Richard Rodgers that felt like a racial milestone to me. I starred opposite James Earl Jones as a poor Harlem single mother in a movie called *Claudine,* and played a well-intentioned stepmother in *Roots: The Next Generations.* I even found my way back to Broadway as a psychiatrist in *Agnes of God.* And all the while, even when others might have allowed themselves to slow down, I kept touring with my nightclub act, keeping my name out there even long into middle age. Then, in 1985, something surprising happened. Aaron Spelling cast me as Dominique Deveraux, the black bitch on *Dynasty.* Not bad at all!

All of the above and much more happened in my first half century. I mean, I once had armed bodyguards in Havana escorting me to perform after Fidel Castro had taken over the government! So I'd say I packed it in. And for each and every performance (and each and every wedding, for that matter), I was always on time, always prepared, and always, *always* coiffed and dressed.

So that spring night not long ago in Manhattan, when I was stepping out of my hotel on Central Park South, belonged as much to me as to anyone in the city. My pants were creamy white and flowing—with flares that were so outrageously wide they flapped as I strode down the steps. I may be a senior, but when it comes to fashion, I try to stay in touch with what's current, as I have done my whole life, ever since my mother took me shopping at Best & Company department store for versions of the clothes showing on the runways. And what good were my superb clothes that night without the right shoes? Mine were something. Aubergine leather boots—with very high heels, as au courant as they were uncomfortable. And also my downfall, literally. As I negotiated the last steps to the sidewalk and town car that would take me on my way, my pointy-toe boot caught in my voluminous flare, and I tripped and went down to the ground.

Brian Panella, my manager, yelled, "Are you all right?" I told him, "Of course I am," and I stood up and kept going. Still, it was an unsettling moment. About to turn seventy, I, a woman who has been wearing heels her whole life, had unceremoniously gone down in them in public.

Did I now have to give up high heels or risk more serious falls in years to come?

You cannot be a legitimate nightclub performer, as far as I'm concerned, in sensible shoes. To me, high heels have always been symbols of sensuality. It's not just about attracting the opposite sex (although I'm never one to say that isn't important). I just know most women look better in high heels. The posture is better, the line of the leg is enhanced. It's more attractive. Even when I have small dinner parties at home, I prefer to wear my heels. I like the way I feel in them. And when you become a senior citizen, there's great pleasure to be had in the fact that even when the tummy isn't as taut as it used to be, the legs are still shapely and slender. They really are the last things to go, you know.

I'm told I look pretty good for my age, with, I am un-ashamed to admit, a little help from my plastic surgeon. When you get to be seventy-three (and by the way, I never lie about my age, but that doesn't mean you're allowed to ask, either!), you know so much more about your life than you did when you're in the thick of things, running the hamster wheel and gathering every damn nut you can. Yes, I'm ambitious, a rampant career-ist who is as dedicated and vain as any performer in the busi-ness. I don't know if that will ever change. But I do feel a shift in myself these days. And even as the legs hang on, the memories fade. So it's nice to have a chance here to look back as a wiser (but not too wizened) person.

That's why I'm writing this book. It isn't the definitive autobiography. I published one of those in 1986, when I was on national television on *Dynasty*. I was having a big moment then, recognized everywhere I went, just like the days when I was *Julia*. But did I ever take a moment to breathe and sit back and enjoy the gift of *Dynasty* giving me a leading role in a successful television show in my middle age, something no actress should take for granted? No. I was too involved in the business of being and promoting Diahann Carroll to step back and admit I wasn't likely to enjoy anything as major as that again.

Let's not be coy. My first fifty years were a dazzling, dizzying ride that included moments with everyone from Miles Davis, Richard Rodgers, and Barbra Streisand to JFK, LBJ, and Jackie O. There was even a lovely proposal of marriage from David Frost. Nothing came easily in my work—I doubt it does to any entertainer, especially an African-American woman from Harlem. But things did come to me, extraordinary opportunities in my first half century. The past twenty years haven't been uneventful, either. Since *Dynasty,* and my last book, wonderful things have continued to come. Some have been on stage and screen. How could I not be thrilled with the chance to be the first black Norma Desmond in the musical *Sunset Boulevard* (at age sixty) or to have a great recurring role for a season of *Grey's Anatomy* ten years later? Getting a rave review in the *New York Times* for my one-woman show a few years back at Feinstein's, a premier cabaret venue in Manhattan, was no small feat, either. But, when all is said and done, those aren't, in my mind, the biggest standouts of these last twenty years.

Since turning fifty (that's when the AARP considers you eligible for membership, just so you know), I've been in and out of my fourth and last marriage (Vic Damone), battled breast cancer, and reconciled with both my father and my daughter. (All that devotion to my work took a toll on my family life.) I helped my mother through her final years on this earth, and came to love her in a way I never imagined I would. I downsized my life and my expectations, performing in more intimate venues than I've seen since my early years of performing, and as difficult as it was, I traded in my Rolls-Royce for a normal sedan. I even had an estate sale and moved out of a spacious

Beverly Hills home to a high-rise condominium. And strange as this sounds, it is only in these golden years that I am finally reveling in the pleasures of family and friendship, as well as the benefits of solitude. I finally see that I no longer need a man to feel I am loved. That is the enormous gift of a lesson that the ending of my fourth marriage gave me.

But then, the big gift of aging is that you are finally in a place where you can understand things you never understood. And with this new equanimity comes perspective and a chance to clear the air, reconcile, laugh, and move on. Finally I understand what it means not to take every damn thing so seriously.

Every week I have to face another shift that tests my ability to laugh at myself. Then I tell myself I have to adjust, and I do. At first, I thought I'd call this book *Too Old to Give a Damn: Things I Never Could Have Said While Working in Hollywood.* I'm no pushover, but I do have the kind of manners that have made me hold back frequently in my lifetime. Then I realized that show business isn't the sole preoccupation of my life any-more. Right now it's about the people I love—here and now—in my golden years. The other day I was on the campus of the University of California–Los Angeles when a shy student approached and asked if I was the actress who played the mom on *Grey's Anatomy.* I told her I was. She told me how much she loved my character, a no-nonsense mother of the doctor played by Isaiah Washington. "You were great, you were right on it," this student told me. Now I would be a disingenuous fool if I were to say that that kind of recognition means nothing to me, especially this late in my life. And I wouldn't be telling the whole story if I also didn't admit that quite regularly strangers come up to me to ask, "Who are you?" At times, I'd like to tell them, "Me? I'm not sure!" After all, all my life people have been trying to make me define myself racially, politically, and artistically. Now they are just trying to place my face. Not long ago, I was standing with Dionne Warwick at a party when someone asked her who her friend was. Did it bother me? Well, maybe a little. He returned shortly thereafter and said, "I know who you are—you're Julia!" But I understand I can't rely on universal recognition anymore for my sense of self-worth. I'm just happy that people in the business still think of me from time to time, and call. I guess that's the payoff for keeping my act together, both figuratively and literally.

Meanwhile, it's the recognition of my grandchildren that really matters to me now. I never thought I'd feel such joy with my family; they have become the world to me. The other day, when I was on the phone with my daughter, she said my granddaughter was waiting to speak to me. She wanted to tell me about her visit to the symphony. I was all ears, hanging on every delicious word. It is wonderful to see my daughter enjoying the relationship I have with her children. It's something I wish I had had with her when she was young. But I was focused, too much so, on my career. Well, it's never too late, I hope.

So do the things that happen late in life really give you the perspective you've been waiting for? Who knows. But the other day, I was attending a benefit when a young black actress asked, "Where have you been?" It made me happy to know she was thinking of me while in the prime of her own career. Well, I'm still here, performing my musical one-woman show at any venue that makes sense to me. And like all actresses of a certain age, I'm still hoping that someone comes along with a script too wonderful to resist. But I'll be honest with you: if you want to know where I am most of the time these days, I'm often enjoying a good book, or with my daughter's family, or out to dinner with friends. It's nice to finally understand that I've had a good run of a life. Now I just have to hope that what I put out there in my career is something that younger actors can still draw upon today. Whenever I find myself around young actors such as Halle Berry and Angela Bassett, they tell me how inspiring my work is to them. And not long ago, Whoopi Goldberg even told me, "I have to thank you for dressing the way you do because you made it okay for me not to worry about what I wear." I'll take that as a compliment.

Maybe this book is my way of having *my* say, just as the Delany sisters had theirs. (In 1999, I played Sadie Delany and the incomparable Ruby Dee played my sister. What a joy it was to work with her. But imagine my shock when I saw what I might look like at age one hundred!) Maybe writing this book is my way of conceding that I'm a little wiser now than I am slim, a little more willing to be amused than I am to be swept off my feet.

But that doesn't mean I can't be the style-conscious shopper I've always been. That's just too much fun to give up.

Superficial, you think? Deeply!

But that's showbiz, and that's me.

ONE

Upon the Wicked Stage

CALL ME CRAZY, BUT I UNDERSTAND NORMA DES-
mond, the silent-screen diva who the world passed by in *Sunset Boulevard*. Norma Desmond drives a Rolls-Royce. Norma Desmond has a penchant for spending lavishly. She knows the magic of makeup and the thrill of casting spells over millions. She is a character who remembers what it's like to be adored when young. She also knows the savagery of show business.

And so do I.

Not that I've had it bad. How many actresses receive a call at fifty to play an overdressed black bitch on an international hit show like *Dynasty*? People still manage to keep me in mind, even now, twenty years later. I get my share of calls to sing in lovely venues, and still know the pleasure of standing on a well-lit stage performing. Sometimes, I am invited to accept an award. But that doesn't mean there aren't plenty of days when I feel completely passed over and passed by. Well, I imagine that's how many people feel when their high-powered careers slow down. Performers, of course, have to deal with droughts and doubts all the time, even when young. It's a tough field. You're in, you're out. You're right for something, you're wrong. You have to learn to live with rejection and curdled ambition on a daily basis, especially if you happen to be female.

Norma Desmond took her discomfort to an epic level. Yet what actress of a certain age would not cringe at the famous Rolls-Royce scene? Norma has finally gotten the call she's been longing for from an accomplished director. She prepares for weeks for her meeting with him—massages, facials, exercise—everything she can do to set back the clock and dazzle when she returns to the lights and cameras. When she finally arrives on the set, in all her glamour and glory, she is quietly hit with the terrible, insulting news that the movie studio has only called her because it wants to use her car, not her, for a movie. It has come to that. Her car is more in demand than she is.

When, in 1994, my agent called to tell me I'd been invited by the producers to audition for Sir Andrew Lloyd Webber's *Sunset Boulevard*, I was familiar with the rhythms of a life in which the phone didn't ring as often, at least not with offers for major roles. I was, after all, in my sixties at the time, and fully aware of the limited shelf life of any acting career. Happily, my emotional footing was far more secure than Norma Desmond's. I knew I wasn't being handed the role. I'd have to work to get it.

I started preparing with even more diligence than usual. And a few days into it, I was told that Sir Andrew was actually going to be at the audition. It was very nerve-racking. Auditioning always is. You have to find the character in your head, and worry if what you find will complement what the director, producer, and writer envision.

I go through this every time I audition. Even after NBC hired me to play Julia, a nurse and single mother, Hal Kanter, the creator of the show, had reservations. He was a charming and outspoken white Southerner who'd been a writer for *Amos 'n' Andy,* among many other projects, and he had a firm sense of what Middle America wanted for its first African-American sitcom star in 1968. And despite the network's faith in me, Hal was not completely convinced that I was the right woman for the role. He felt my image was too worldly and glamorous.

Well, I had won a Tony for playing a chic model in Paris for Richard Rodgers on Broadway, and I had done several Hollywood films with Otto Preminger. I performed in luxurious venues in New York, Las Vegas, and Miami, and had appeared on beautifully produced television specials for years. I was one of those fortunate performers—and there might have been only a dozen of us in total—who went from show to show—*Ed Sullivan, Dean Martin, Judy Garland*—holiday specials, shows about everything from Broadway to black humor. I was even chosen in 1967 to costar with Maurice Chevalier in the first collaboration between French and American television. Every appearance was more lavish than the next.

Hal Kanter knew all about my jet-set lifestyle when NBC told him he was to meet with me. I knew about his hesitancy, so for our first meeting, I dressed carefully—to look modest, and though it was a Givenchy, the line was so simple, I knew it would work—and walked into the Polo Lounge of the Beverly Hills Hotel.

I was told later that he didn't recognize me. "That's the look I want for this character," he told a colleague. "A well-dressed housewife just like that woman."

Then I came over to the table and he discovered that "that woman" was me.

"Hal," I said. "I know I can do this. I'm an actress. You saw me come through that door and I convinced you that I could be a housewife. Well, guess what? I *prepared* to be a housewife for this interview. And I think this is how Julia would dress."

I have to say, preparing to audition for Norma Desmond was less of a stretch. Although I've always considered myself more of a worker than a diva, I could relate to the character of an extravagant actress in the twilight of her career. I felt so much pressure for my *Sunset Boulevard* audition. I knew I was the first black actress to be considered for the role, and worked very hard to keep that thought out of my head as I rehearsed with my pianist. I was intent on nailing the character of a sixty-year-old woman living in complete denial, no matter what color she is.

In situations like that, one question rises to the surface above all others: *What the hell am I going to wear?* The day of the audition, I changed outfits several times and left clothes all over my bedroom, as if I were a teenager on a first date.

Finally I decided that the most dramatic look (that wouldn't come off as being stark raving mad) was a white ensemble—white trousers, white blouse, and to really push it, a white Burberry raincoat. Then, to take it up another notch, I added a white fedora. It was very dramatic, if not completely obsessive. But then, I am one of those people who cannot leave the house without overthinking an outfit. I looked anything but casual.

I made a decision that I would drive myself that day rather than use a driver. I arrived at the Shubert Theater in Century City to be greeted by the pianist I was to work with, a lovely young man named Paul. "Miss Carroll, it's so wonderful," he said. "Sir Andrew is in town and he wants to hear you sing!" Now I knew some of the history of this production. I knew that Glenn Close was playing Norma Desmond in Los Angeles, and that Betty Buckley was playing her in New York. I also knew that Faye Dunaway had cost the producers a good deal of money in a role that ended up not being right for her. Lastly, I knew that the job I was up for was not in the New York or Los Angeles productions, but in Toronto. If I got the part, I'd be living there at least a year.

It didn't matter. I wanted to play Norma Desmond.

The agreement for the audition was that I would work with the pianist provided by the producers for forty-five minutes so that we could find our way through the song I had chosen to sing, which was the beautiful main ballad from the show, "As If We Never Said Goodbye." Usually I bring my own pianist, with whom I've prepared extensively. This was a different situation, one that made me a little uncomfortable. But I started to work with Paul, and it was going well, when the door to the rehearsal room burst open. It was Sir Andrew himself. He strode up to us, waved his hand at the pianist, and said, "I'll take over, I'll do this with her." My heart started pounding. The pianist looked at me and I looked at him with complete terror in my eyes.

Sir Andrew threw himself down at the piano and played a chord or two. Then he looked up at me and said, with his arch and intimidating English accent, "So sing something!"

"Sing something?" I repeated.

"Sing anything. How about 'Melancholy Baby'?"

I said, " 'Melancholy Baby'? Why?"

"Why not?" he said.

"Is this a show about a saloon?" I found myself continuing. "Can we maybe try a love song instead, something that isn't too difficult, like 'More Than You Know'?"

"No, I don't know that," he said.

I could instantly see that he was not to be spoken to like that, worker to worker. So even as I tried to remain calm my nerves started fraying. I'd worked with composers my whole life, and they were almost always wonderful to me, nurturing and open-minded, treating me as if I were a colleague, not an employee. I had never come across anyone who behaved like the "star creator." Harold Arlen, one of our greatest composers, was so modest and sweet. He never tried to impress or impose.

After a few disagreeable minutes of having to hold my ground and not sing a saloon song, Sir Andrew said to me, "Well, what is it that you came prepared to sing?"

I told him it was the ballad "As If We Never Said Goodbye" from his show.

"All right, then why don't you go ahead and sing it?"

He played a few bars. I could tell the key was not in my vocal register.

"I'm afraid that isn't my key," I said.

"Well, give it a try anyway," he said. "Let's hear what you can do."

That key he selected was more likely to showcase what I *couldn't* do. I could not believe this was happening. But I would not capitulate, either. I had not spent all these many years in my profession only to be denied what was due to me. I suspected that Sir Andrew was unhappy with me for being a singer who played Vegas more often than Broadway. And although I had not given it any thought, I suddenly couldn't help wondering if behind this complete disregard for the basic courtesy due a performer was a creator of a show who was perhaps a little dubious about casting a black actress as Norma Desmond. Let me be clear. Casting is a taste business, so any number of reasons can form a decision. And this was not obvious racism. I'd seen that at work. Obvious racism is when people yell terrible remarks while you're singing, as they did when I played nightclubs in my early years. Out-and-out racism is when the Count Basie Orchestra is not allowed to stay at a hotel in Las Vegas in the 1950s until Frank Sinatra himself has to explain to management that the Basie orchestra has to be housed at the hotel where he was living. Obvious racism is when the sponsor of a 1968 Petula Clark television special tries to delete a moment when she affectionately touches Harry

Belafonte's arm because bodily contact was deemed unacceptable between races.

Obvious racism is when a cabdriver noticed I was black after he'd stopped for me in front of my apartment on Riverside Drive many years ago, and started driving away with me holding on to the door handle. I was being dragged down the street. The doormen on both sides of my street came running over to my aid. When I stood up, they asked if I was okay.

"I'm fine, but I have to have his number to report him," I said.

The doormen helped a moment before disappearing. Clearly, they didn't want to get involved. So I took off my kid gloves, got a pen out of my Kelly bag, and took down the cab number. As I was doing so, the driver said, "What are you going to do? Report me? All that means is I lose a day."

"We'll see," I said as I finished writing his number down.

"Why waste your time and my time?" he said, snickering.

Because he needed to see that I took his racism seriously, that's why. I took him to court downtown, a place I'd been several times before to report taxis that had not picked me up. And he was docked five days, an order I knew he didn't actually have to adhere to. But I felt much better knowing that cabdrivers in that courtroom that day realized that some people of color will not allow that kind of behavior.

Of course that was nothing compared with what I experienced years before, in 1957, when I was singing in Lake Tahoe at a hotel. It was early in my career and I was not traveling

with my own musicians. On our first night, the orchestra conductor began to get closer to me onstage. He backed up and
was right alongside me. I looked at him as if to say, "Why are
you standing next to me?" I was the star singer, and he was
supposed to be conducting the orchestra, not moving closer to
the audience into my spotlight. It seemed to me he was trying
to tell me he did not want to be in the position of conducting
for me. But I didn't say anything. After the second night of
this same strange usurping of my space, I approached him
after the show and asked what had happened. The entire orchestra was listening.

"What was it? Did you have trouble hearing me?" I asked.

He didn't answer. But the next night he did the same thing,
backing into my spotlight again. I was performing in my demure gown and pearls, and he was in a white dinner jacket,
shoulder to shoulder with me, waving his arms around, conducting. It was a complete distraction and completely unacceptable. While the audience was applauding me I turned to ask
him in a stage whisper, "Why are you standing next to me? I
don't understand."

That's when he snapped, "These people don't want to hear
a nigger sing."

Then he turned to start the orchestra on the next song,
and feeling winded, I took a breath and went on to sing my
Ethel Waters medley.

Backstage later, I asked the members of the orchestra if
they heard his remark.

"Yes, we did," one musician said.

"We've been waiting for you to find out," said another. "He can't stand the fact that he has to conduct for you. He's a nasty racist and he especially hates black people." I stood there, stunned, reminding myself not to allow this ignorant man to force me to behave inappropriately, so slapping his face was out of the question! "Oh," I said quietly in front of the musicians, who looked very uncomfortable. "Well, I'll have to see what I can do about this."

Several musicians told me that anything I wanted to do, they would support. They had traveled around the country too often not to know there were all kinds of problems of prejudice that musicians had to face, not just as artists but as Jews, Italians, and Hispanics. And they did not understand how anyone in their own profession, a fellow artist, could be so provincial and hateful. I called the police and the union.

The police took my report. "Have you been harmed?" they asked.

"No," I told them, "but I've been the target of racist slurs."

I had not decided if I'd even go on to perform the next night until I learned what response I would get from the phone calls I'd made. The union contacted me, then contacted the conductor and threatened him, and that frightened him. So he came into my dressing room.

"What did you tell these people?" he said with a laugh.

"That you told me the audience doesn't want to hear a nigger sing," I said.

"Oh, come on." He snickered. "You know I was only joking."

I said, "Well, I'll tell you what we're going to do. You are going to apologize to me in front of the entire orchestra for joking in such a way."

"Are you crazy?" he asked.

"If you don't," I said, "I will not perform."

He shook his head as if I were out of my mind.

But I went ahead and gathered the orchestra into the rehearsal room. And the conductor, who I later learned had been a member of the Little Rascals (he played Porky), stood there with me and said something like, "Diahann Carroll here is accusing me of racist remarks." He didn't say he was sorry for his behavior.

"But actually," I said, "I would like you to apologize to me and to all of us. Your remark was an insult to what we do."

He just laughed at me, shook his head, and walked out.

I asked the musicians, "So what do I do now? The only thing I can do is quit."

We gathered in my hotel room for a meeting. We all agreed that we would all suffer if I didn't go on with my booking. Nobody would get paid. There was no way around it. So I simply asked to have this man removed from my show. An assistant conducted instead. It's not a big payoff ending, but it took care of the problem at hand.

That was real racism. What I was facing with Sir Andrew Lloyd Webber wasn't anything in that league. He had mentioned at some point during our awkward meeting that no silent-screen stars were black. And I told him there was no Norma Desmond, either. "She's a fictional character," I said. But I still don't know to this day why he was so keen on maligning me at that audition when he saw me becoming so anxious in his presence.

"All right, so I'll give you a chord, now go ahead and sing," he was telling me.

"But I was told I could rehearse with a pianist before presenting it," I said.

"What do you mean?" he said briskly. "Come on. Just sing it. Just sing!"

I was completely unmoored now. And quite frankly, I figured at this point he didn't want to work with me if I was being so difficult. So my dream of getting this part was pretty much falling apart. But I did not break out into a sweat and feel my throat go dry. I knew what I had been promised. I had been told that I would have forty-five minutes to work with a pianist before singing for the producers, director, and creator of the show. Finally they phoned my agent and he defended my contractual agreement in no uncertain terms. He suggested they let me go home. "So you really won't sing?" Sir Andrew asked.

"I will," I said. "And I'm sorry, but I really want to have a moment to prepare."

And with that, I was shown the door. The rehearsal pianist walked me out of the dark theater into the parking lot and accompanied me to my car, a Rolls. It was champagne- and chocolate-colored, and looking regal in a lonely, sunlit lot.

"That's not your car, is it?" he said.

"Yes," I said. "That's my car."

He shook his head and laughed. It was just too Norma Desmond.

"I have driven a Rolls for years," I said.

To be honest, I was a little embarrassed. On the one hand, a Rolls is a power statement in a town in which dropping off and picking up at valet parking is a form of ritual display. But on the other hand, I knew that driving one when I was not at the top of anyone's list anymore was a slightly dangerous choice of statement making, and more than a little "Norma Desmond" in the eyes of the all-knowing types in Los Angeles.

Sending the wrong message can get you in trouble in this town. And the worst message of all is when you're driving a fancy car that is in need of repair.

In 1976, I was truly wondering where my life was going. My hit albeit controversial series *Julia* was long over. So was my summer television series, *The Diahann Carroll Show. Dynasty* was in the future, but I had no idea of that then. Show business had already started to change, and singers like me who loved nothing more than performing the standards of the older generation were being challenged by everything from the Bee Gees to Motown. Around that time, I remember quite clearly the sight of a bright yellow Bentley convertible coming at me on Coldwater Canyon Drive in Beverly Hills. I had never seen such a color in my life except on a taxicab in New York. Behind the wheel of this lurid yellow car was this tiny black woman with a huge head of hair flying in the wind. As she drove past me, I recognized it was Diana Ross.

"There goes the neighborhood," I muttered to myself.

Now, I know that sounds terrible. But you have to understand that in 1976, a bright yellow Bentley (or was it a

Rolls?) was as out of place as Albert Einstein might have been in this town. And there's no denying that I was just learning what to make of the influence of Motown on the music industry. I knew it was brilliant, but I simply couldn't relate to it. I was immersed in an old-fashioned notion of elegance and sophistication and had no choice but to remain true to the music of Gershwin, Porter, and Ellington—what I knew and was raised on. All this new music represented a loss of footing for me. Yes, I'll admit it, I was confused about Detroit, too. I was, after all, from New York, the apex of all things sophisticated, cultural, and old school. And like so many transplants, I was very defensive about giving up Manhattan for Los Angeles. So as I drove past that huge flashy yellow convertible, I probably didn't want to admit how worried I was about my own career.

It had not gone as well as I had hoped after three seasons of *Julia*. My summer variety show was successful and paid well, but it had come and gone, and it seemed to me that the era of lavish television specials was coming to an end. I was convinced that there was less demand for a chanteuse like me, a girl who became a singing star on television and in nightclubs wearing pearls. There was more interest in performers who were more soulful. The great Aretha Franklin. The singular Nina Simone. Our culture was rapidly changing and I knew I had to rethink my situation. Norma Desmond was appealing to act onstage, but in real life I had to embrace the new. So I set out to do just that. If I get an A for effort, I don't get such high marks for execution. When I look back on *The Carol Burnett Show* and see myself in a macramé vest and silly hat, singing songs that just didn't come naturally to me, I notice my own awkwardness. I was trying to adapt to the new trends—which change every ten years or so, requiring those of us in the business to keep on our toes—but that was not for me. I was and always will be a chanteuse in the way I understand the term. That was hard to reconcile with the 1970s, an era of strident liberation. The only important film role I played during those years was representative of where the cultural interest was—as a welfare mother in the independent film *Claudine.* She was gritty, real, an honest black woman working her tail off. It was a great part. But no other roles were forthcoming, so I continued to travel. But in this new world, could I really still afford my Rolls and my mansion in Benedict Canyon with a wine cellar, waterfall, and three-car garage?

Harry Belafonte had advised me to always make the best financial deal I possibly could, because no career is guaranteed, especially for an African-American woman in showbiz. He also explained early on in my career that touring, regardless of how inconvenient it was, could be very lucrative. That's why when Richard Rodgers's *No Strings* was ready for its national tour, I decided to go with it.

I remember the day I had a horrifically unsettling experience in a department store. It was in the early 1980s, and I had driven my Rolls to Saks Fifth Avenue in Beverly Hills. I did not give much thought to the fact that it needed some work. Usually I'm persnickety, but around this time, I'd been neglectful. So the Rolls wasn't looking its best that day. Anyway, I had bought some bathing suits and cover-ups for a trip, and while I was in the dressing room, a young salesclerk came in to see me.

"Miss Carroll," she said. "Your credit card didn't go through."

I stood there, confused. I had never heard those words before, ever. It was so mortifying I hardly knew what to say. Then, as I stepped out of the dressing room, there were some women who wanted my autograph. Can you imagine? I signed for them and spoke in a way that was more animated than usual. Then I called over to the clerk, "I'll be back to take care of this tomorrow!" I wanted to make it clear to everyone in that swimsuit department at Saks that I did not have a financial problem. And I actually didn't. It was more that I was starting to feel a kind of slipping from the top of the food chain at the time. Certainly, I could pay my bills. But I probably couldn't continue to travel the way I traveled, extravagantly, with twenty pieces of luggage and an entourage. In my midforties, I was beginning to make contact with the feeling that my life had changed, and that I might not be able to maintain the level of success that had come so easily in the past. Should I really be driving a Rolls, particularly one in need of a few repairs? My outspoken agent, Roy Gerber, didn't think so. He told me that someone had cringed seeing me pull up to the Beverly Wilshire for lunch.

"My friend saw you get out of your car and he called me immediately," Roy told me. "He said you should stop driving it because it's a perfect example of someone having financial problems." I finally got it repaired, and I kept trading up for new ones, just as my father had done with his Chryslers all my childhood. And now, fifteen years later, here I was after a disastrous audition, standing in a theater parking lot about to get into my Rolls, and worrying about how to pay for my life. I didn't just want to play Norma Desmond in the national production of *Sunset Boulevard* in Toronto. I *had* to.

I unlocked the door to the car and got in.

"I just can't believe this is really your car," the pianist said.

"Well, I promised myself years ago that I would drive a Rolls all my life," I told him. "It's very important to me that I only have the best for myself and my child."

He nodded respectfully, and then shook his head.

"Well, I wish those people inside that theater could see you now, because quite clearly you *are* Norma Desmond," he said. "You have the perfect voice, looks, and car."

I thanked him and drove away, angry that the revered creator of the show could feel it was his right to tease me and try to provoke me into singing saloon songs. And I was upset that I was not the kind of person who could joke around with him and go with the flow. My whole life I've been careful and formal. The only time I wasn't was when I ran in for my second audition for *House of Flowers* with a crazy, chopped-off hairstyle, so exhausted that without even thinking, I sat down on the edge of the stage, kicked off my shoes, and sang to Harold Arlen, Truman Capote, and all the producers in the dark. But I was a girl then, barely twenty years old. Now I was very much an adult.

"Well, that's that," I said as I drove home. So much for *Sunset Boulevard*.

Not long after that, my agent got another call, and I was sent some music to prepare and asked to fly to Toronto. After another audition, without Sir Andrew around, I was granted my proper time with a rehearsal pianist and sang well. The producer, Garth Drabinksy, told me he had wanted me all along. No, Sir Andrew was not totally happy about the choice. I don't think he wanted me at all, and claimed that I couldn't sing in the key in which the songs were written. But the final decision about me was the producer's, not the creator's. And I was offered the job that very day, and like any woman in her sixties, I was terribly delighted to be wanted again.

But it didn't take long to realize that I was back in the theater, and that meant I would be locked away day in and day out in my own little gilded cage. I always took my work so seriously, too seriously. For an entire year, I would be committed to eight shows a week, worrying about my throat, with humidifiers all around me. But I desperately needed to prove I could play the role. I was the oldest woman to play Norma Desmond, and certainly the darkest. My leading man, Rex Smith, was very charming and extremely talented. And there was something so rewarding about not having to worry for two years about what kind of jobs I might be offered.

The revolving set for the show was incredibly ornate and so were the costumes. Sweeping around in capes as heavy as velvet drapes and walking up and down three hundred steps eight performances weekly in heels and a leopard-skin gown that weighed sixty pounds almost killed me. One night I tripped and injured my ankle badly. I iced it in between scenes so the show could go on. That's the reality of live theater. It can be painful and it isn't always pretty. Yet it can be so rewarding.

The reviews and audiences were wonderful. Toronto's a beautiful city and its theatergoers are as sophisticated as any in the world. And if the American press didn't pay much attention to the production, I was just becoming seasoned enough to understand that less than perfect can be good enough. You learn that as you age, I think—to appreciate fully what you're given. It's a kind of acceptance that can bring peace, even to an overly ambitious perfectionist like me.

The one thing that I could not accept from my experience as the lead in Toronto's *Sunset Boulevard* was the night Sir Andrew came from England to see our performance. The company was thrilled that we would be able to meet the great creator of so many shows and songs we knew so well. The plan was that we'd have some time with him after the show. So after the curtain fell, we were all racing around in our dressing rooms, pulling ourselves together for our moment. But then his voice came over our PA system, sounding brittle and rushed.

"Thank you all so very much for a lovely performance. I enjoyed it very much. My pilot has just informed me that the skies are clouding over and that I must leave immediately, but again, thank you for a fine show." There was dead silence everywhere.

We had all worked so hard on this show and we were really disappointed. The cast so wanted to meet him, be around him for a half hour. That's how actors are. We try our best to interpret the work of important artists every single night, and it would have just been so wonderful to be able to greet him. I was also looking forward to burying any ill will between us. But he was gone, just gone. I was demolished and demoralized. You do feel responsible for the company when you're the star of the show. And I just couldn't believe he would do that.

On the other hand, I'd been the leading lady in a similar situation years ago with the great Richard Rodgers. Actually, it was worse.

It happened in Detroit. I was working extremely hard in 1962 for the out-of-town opening of the Broadway-bound *No Strings*. And the night before we opened, Mr. Rodgers came to see me in my dressing room. In a voice that was something between avuncular and condescending, he told me he had something he needed to discuss with me: the hostess of our opening-night party did not want me in her home. She felt that it would confuse her children to see a black woman who was sophisticated and elegant because they didn't exist. She told Rodgers she was certain he'd hired tutors to teach me diction and manners, and that I was a fabricated black character who was designed to startle white audiences. Did Rodgers, who wrote "You've Got to Be Carefully Taught" about prejudice for *South Pacific,* argue with this racist hostess or give her a dressing-down? Did he tell her to cancel her party? No, he did neither. Well, I'd seen him be cruel in the past. Once in his office, he referred to Larry Hart, one of his former collaborators, as a fag. Another time, I ran into him in front of our hotel, again while we were trying out *No Strings* in Detroit. It was a rainy day, and when he asked how I was doing, I told him I was having a terrible time getting a cab. He said, "Oh, that's too bad," and then went and left in his limo without offering me a ride to the theater. It amazes me when people who have the ability to create such beautiful music can behave so rudely.

At any rate, when he told me that I would not be invited to the cast party, I wasn't really surprised. After all, when you live a life in which racial prejudice is a daily experience, you carry with you a mental first-aid kit to fix any situation to avoid further infection of your soul. So I had my assistant call a favorite restaurant across the street from our theater, and reserved it for our private party. Everyone in the cast and crew was invited. We had a ball. We ate and drank, hugging one another and praising one another and giving one another the kind of support we needed after so many weeks of difficult rehearsals. And I never chose to speak of the incident again with Mr. Rodgers. I have never understood the point of dwelling on things that are so blatantly obvious. And besides, I could not withdraw from the theater opportunity of a lifetime.

Mr. Rodgers had called me on the telephone to introduce the idea of *No Strings* in 1961. He had loved my work in Capote and Arlen's *House of Flowers,* and a few years later, in 1957, had tried to make me up to look Asian for *Flower Drum Song,* a look that didn't work. I knew he had wanted to work with me for years, and I was excited. The morning he called was after one of my appearances on *The Tonight Show* with Jack Paar, where I was becoming a regular—a great boon to my public profile. For my meeting with Mr. Rodgers, I went in a pale pink Givenchy suit and pillbox hat. It was a perfect choice. "You look marvelous," he said. "That's exactly how I want you to look onstage in my show." And so I did. In *No Strings,* I played an American model in Paris who falls in love with an American writer played by Richard Kiley. We have a glorious, glamorous fling (that only ends when he has to go back to the States) in a bonbon of a beautifully designed show. It meant the world to be able to depict a black woman with some sophistication, and it was especially gratifying to know I was part of the first integrated love affair on Broadway. This was Rodgers's first project without a lyricist, it was a solid hit, and I won a Tony Award. My competitors for the prize in 1962 were Anna Marie Alberghetti, Molly Picon, and Elaine Stritch.

And *No Strings* was an almost perfect experience. I say almost perfect because show business is never without its regrettable moments. The cast party in Detroit was one. The other came in the days after I received my Tony Award, and I opened the papers to find out that Nancy Kwan, an Asian-American actress, had been cast to play my role in the Warner Brothers film version of the show. Yes, Audrey Hepburn had replaced Julie Andrews for the film version of *My Fair Lady,* just as Andrews would replace Mary Martin for the film version of *The Sound of Music.* But this was different. I wasn't too old for the part in the movie, just too black. Around that time, I had testified for Adam Clayton Powell Jr. about limited opportunities for black performers. In the wake of the news about *No Strings,* the NAACP sent a petition to Warner Bros., demanding to know how many black people it employed. Several groups threatened to boycott the film. The studio eventually decided to shelve the project.

It was devastating to be unwelcome at a cast party and the movie version of a show that had been written for me. But by then, I already knew how cruel show business could be. The great Pearl Bailey was the one who taught me my very first lesson about these immense cruelties in show business. In *House of Flowers,* she played a madam in a West Indian bordello who helps raise Ottilie, the young ingenue I was playing. Despite all odds (and sense, when I look back on it now), Ottilie remains lovely, innocent, and pure.

I was nineteen at the time, and looked rather innocent myself. I suppose that's why Pearl became so maternal. I don't think she knew that I didn't really need any mothering, given that I had such an attentive and loving mother. But Pearl was very sweet to me. Then, suddenly she wasn't. We were still in rehearsals on the road. And on the show's opening night in Philadelphia, I decided to apply a little eyeliner on my eyelids so the audience would notice my eyes, a standard routine for any theater actress. But before the curtain went up, and in the kind of loud, dramatic voice I had worked to eliminate from my own persona, I heard her on the other side of the theater. The whole cast and crew heard her, too. "That girl is covered in makeup," she was yelling. "This show will not go on until she removes every last bit of it, do you hear me?" To be honest, I didn't even know whom she was talking about. So I couldn't believe it when the stage manager walked over to me, and with a sheepish voice said I'd have to wash my face. It was mortifying. But I didn't argue. I knew what was going on. She was threatened by my youth, and wanted to keep me as barefoot and dowdy as possible.

"So that's what it means to be the star," I told myself as I washed my face.

Then it got worse. I had a beautiful song in the show called "Don't Like Goodbyes." It was Harold Arlen at his finest, and the audience was wild for the song. After a performance in our out-of-town rehearsals, there was a knock on my door. The producer, Saint-Suber, and Mr. Arlen were standing there. He was a terribly dapper-looking man, but he was also nurturing, and spoke to performers with respect and kindness. This was, in fact, a man whose personality was equal to the loving and idealistic songs he wrote.

"This is going to sound awful, and it isn't very pleasant, so get ready," he said. "And I have to apologize because we never should have allowed this to happen."

My heart skipped several beats. What could this be? I knew I wasn't being fired.

Then the producer quietly said, "We're going to have to take the song 'Don't Like Goodbyes' away from you. Pearl wants to sing it."

I didn't say what I wanted to say, which was, "Are you all crazy?"

I might have suggested that the song would make no sense if her character sang it. But I knew the rules well by then—don't argue with the star. So I didn't cry or carry on at all. I simply told myself that there was nothing to be done about this situation. If there's something that you can do, then you have to fight for it. Or maybe you get the people you are paying to do the fighting for you. But this? Nothing to be done about it. She wanted my song.

So it was decided that to help the song make sense, I would remain onstage as Miss Bailey sang it to me. The director put me at her feet. I was looking out to the audience, wistfully, as she sang:

Don't like goodbyes,
Tears or sighs . . .

She was playing the loving woman who had adopted me, and I was this girl whom she had raised to become a lady. It was decided that I would rest my face on her lap and she would tenderly rub my cheeks and forehead as I looked outward and she sang the song that was one of the most beautiful I'd ever heard, a song that gave me chills when I sang it. But the first night she sang my song, she took my head into both her hands, and slowly but forcefully turned my face completely upstage, away from the audience, and then she buried my face in her ample lap.

I'm not too good at leavin' time . . .
I got no taste for grievin' time

While breathing into the fabric of her dress, I waited for her to lift my face back up so I could continue breathing freely and looking out at the audience. But it soon became clear that she was going to keep my head placed right there where she decided it should be. I wanted to bite her, but I told myself, "You can't change this, leave it alone." And when the song ended, and she had let me go, I heard the audience applaud her instead of me. Everyone tried to convince her it made no sense for her character to sing that song.

"No, it's fine," she said. "We'll leave it just like it is."

So, as I say, show business can be cruel. *Sunset Boulevard* epitomizes that, and Norma Desmond is an example of what it's like to fight with the fact that you are getting older. Well, we do have a terrible problem with age in this country. But you know what? I think it's ridiculous for older women to allow themselves to be so demoralized. Say what you want about Norma, at least she had the wherewithal to try to get someone to write a script for her so she could have a role to play. She did what she could, and only when she realizes that she is no longer wanted, not by Hollywood and not by her young man, does she have her famous "ready for my close-up" meltdown scene. I'm glad that I've figured out at this tender age that public recognition is not the most important thing in life. I'm glad I have friends around to laugh with me and discuss the pros and cons of liposuction and other pertinent issues of the day. It's a lot more fun. On the other hand, imagine how gratifying it was for me, at the end of that show in that theater in Toronto, to stand at the top of a staircase and go stark raving mad? That scene is the perfect fulfillment for any actress who has spent her life in the industry.

Well, in a way, I really was going mad at the time. Things with Vic Damone, my fourth husband, were falling apart. In my *Sunset Boulevard* interviews at the time, I'd joke about how wonderful it was to play Norma Desmond.

"She goes mad and shoots a man eight times a week," I'd say.

I was only half joking.

TWO

Queen Mother

SO HOW DOES A GIRL FROM HARLEM GROW UP TO BE a doyenne of stage, screen, and TV, with a penchant for couture, coiffure, Rolls-Royces, and the great composers of her time? In the tradition of so many memoirs, you can blame it all on my mother. She is the woman who made it her business to nurture me so completely as a child that I felt beautiful and special from the start. She lived a long life. When she died in 1999, I was already in my sixties, a senior citizen myself. The day of her passing, I didn't pause for even a moment to reflect on how important she'd been to me. I didn't cry, either. I simply flew into combat mode, the way I do when I'm pulling one of my shows together for the road, and I started making the funeral arrangements. I told the young woman at the funeral parlor that I would bring in all my mother's personal makeup, everything she had, "And I want you to make her look like a movie star." She never liked having gray hair, but she had no choice but to let it go gray in her last year. So I had it dyed black for the funeral—just the way she liked it. The makeup job was subtle. The color of her outfit was not. I put her in a military red Diahann Carroll suit, a color she always loved in her favorite designer label.

I guess I wasn't, at that moment, able to accept the loss of someone who had always been such a presence in my life. And I wasn't ready to accept the fact that we had all kinds of issues that remained unresolved right to the end. Or perhaps I should say I had all these issues with her that I'd never resolved for my-self. It's strange. I am a woman known in my profession for having a level head. To survive in show business, especially when race is part of the scenario, it helps to keep calm. But just thinking about my mother, all these years after she's gone, still makes me feel flustered, like a child who cannot figure out how to get her point across to the most important person in her life.

"Mom!" I hear myself saying over and over. "You don't understand!"

Are there any more familiar words between mothers and daughters?

Why did I need to harangue her so much, to lecture her about things her old-fashioned soul didn't want to accept? Did I have to hold her responsible for so many of my failings as a woman and a wife? Was it necessary to shake her up with every little thing I'd learned about myself in psychotherapy? And could I not have allowed her a few more indulgences in the accessories department? Maybe I didn't need to tease her quite so much about her big earrings. She was a simple, polite, churchgoing lady who liked to do things properly. Okay, well, maybe not that properly, when the truth came out. But I didn't discover all that about her until much later in our lives. My mother!

She did look fabulous in her casket. I wouldn't have had it any other way.

Some people might say I'm too image-conscious. They don't think that walking around in beaded dresses and heels adds up to a meaningful life. I don't do that every day. But I do it more than your average senior citizen. What can I say? It pleases me to know I've been on the International Best Dressed list twice in my life. I want to make the best entrance I possibly can. Just as I select songs for my cabaret performances carefully, I select wardrobe with great attention to detail. Materialistic? Of course it is. I'm nothing if not materialistic, and have been since I was young. My idea of a good time is shopping, and nobody is going to make me feel guilty about it. And I don't care what today's actresses tell you about having their best times in jeans and T-shirts, they are as image-conscious as those of us who grew up with a more studied idea of style.

Blame it on the movies, if you like. I grew up watching MGM musicals, Joan Crawford, Bette Davis, and Lena Horne, all women who were concerned with looking smashing, not natural. Then there was the woman who schooled me early on in the ways of style—my mother. She was a high-school-educated woman with a highly developed sense of dignity, and she was on a mission to make me aware of how good I looked.

My confidence, my drive, and care about my personal style all come from her.

We didn't have much money, but, oh, did we have style!

My parents were practically children themselves when they met in 1931 at a carnival on Long Island. My father had just come up to New York from Aiken, South Carolina. My mother was just up from Bladenboro, North Carolina, and had been looking for work, with the encouragement of her own hard-working mother, while on her summer vacation. She was twenty-one, he was twenty, and working as a lithographic printer as well as a caddie on Long Island golf courses. He did not have anything beyond an elementary school education, and she only got as far as high school. But they had charming smiles, social grace, a relentless urge to escape the South and improve their lives, and, well, to be frank, a healthy attraction to the opposite sex. They liked each other right away. "That's the man I'm going to marry," my mother told a cousin when she first saw my father.

Mabel Faulk, my mother, was striking. She had great cheekbones, her mother's almond-toned skin, and smoky, intriguing eyes. Her features were well proportioned and she had a shape that was coveted at the time—ample breasts, small waist, and full hips. She was never thin, but always voluptuous, with the most lovely legs. She wore shorts until she was eighty-two years old, bless her, and her hair was always thick and dark. She knew she was attractive and she worked it. Her glance was more solicitous than seductive. At any rate, men always looked.

My father, John Johnson, was always a looker. He was a man's man—tall and solid, and powerful in stature, with warm amber skin, a strong nose and mouth, and piercing, animated eyes. He was never much of a talker. A black boy raised in the South by a quick-tempered father learns how to keep his mouth shut. A black boy who was once almost set on fire by racists in his hometown, learning that he cannot find relief in justice by telling anyone the truth about something so awful, keeps his anger locked inside, and adapts to a world in which to get along, you make yourself as agreeable as possible. At any rate, he was always a charmer, and the ladies always responded.

Well, how do you resist a man in houndstooth pants, a crisp white shirt, and spit-shined wingtip shoes? Even at ninety-six, he was a dignified flirt.

He wasn't looking to settle down when he met my mother but "she was nice, real nice," he liked to say about her with the same sly smile that often appeared when he remembered her. He was just getting used to being on his own, breathing easy, for once in his life, out from under the punitive hand of his father. He and my mother married in 1933, in a small ceremony at Harlem's Abyssinian Baptist Church. The highly influential Reverend Adam Clayton Powell Sr., whose son became the powerful congressman years later, officiated. The newlywed Mr. and Mrs. Johnson were drawn to Harlem, in the heyday of its renaissance. It lured so many young blacks eager to join its rich and vibrant culture. "Back then, it was the only place to be," my father told me.

John found a small apartment for himself and his new bride on West 151st Street, not too far from the storied 409 Edgecombe Avenue, where W. E. B. DuBois and Thurgood Marshall were among the famous tenants. Because my father's salary, as a printer and caddie, was not enough for two, my mother had to find work doing housework. My father couldn't stand the idea of his wife having to work. It was a symbol of his inability to support his family. To him, a man wasn't a man unless he could do that. By his careful calculations, he needed to look for another job.

A year and a half into the marriage, in 1935, I came along. Ta-da. Carol Diann Johnson, a surprise baby. With my arrival, John's search for a better job became urgent. In their brief time together, John had seen Mabel's independence and fiery spirit. When her labor started after an argument, Mabel, in a fit of anger and spite, drove herself to a Bronx hospital to have me. Eventually, John got the call at work, and he had to race uptown to find his wife and greet me properly. My parents really were children in so many ways. Not that I'm one to talk, given my naive ways around men my whole life. But my parents' immaturity eventually did make marriage difficult, especially in later years. Yet they were such a wonderful team, too, from early on.

They were strivers, up-and-comers. My father had set his sights on a better job than working at a printing shop, and wanted to work for the city's subway system, one of the few places a black man could find decent pay, security, and benefits. My mother helped him study for the transit test he had to take. I remember when I was about five, watching them at our kitchen table, the boisterous life of the Harlem streets right outside our window, as they pored over papers with the quiet diligence of scholars. Dad passed the test, and landed a job with benefits, his first, making change in token booths. It was 1940. At the time, a ride cost five cents.

So now my parents, the Johnsons, were moving up in the world. They had a strong desire to live and socialize among the African-American upper crust, who for the most part had parlayed their lighter skin and straighter hair into better opportunities. But unfortunately, in the rarefied world of exclusive black social clubs like The Jack and Jill and The Links, where looks could influence social standing, John and Mabel Johnson were missing the key attribute that would have unlocked all the doors for them. Yes, my mother was light-skinned, and my father could have made it through the "paper-bag test," meaning you could be no darker in skin color than a paper bag, but they did not have that all-essential college education to prove their worth. Without that, they were left on the outside of the Harlem society they craved to join. But their alienation made them determined to see that their own children would not face those kind of barriers and limitations.

They did only one thing in my entire childhood that made me feel unloved. When I was still a toddler, they left me with my mother's sister in North Carolina. To the sound of tree frogs in the hot and humid evening, my mother tucked me in and kissed me good night, and the next morning she was gone. Gone! She and my father had decided that they could not afford to be proper parents and work to earn enough to support us decently. So one morning, with honeybees and crickets now buzzing outside the window of a house with no plumbing or electricity, I awoke to find no mother. My aunt scrubbed me in a big tin washtub. I was utterly bewildered. Why would my mother leave me without even telling me why? Was I too young to understand without flying into a tantrum that would tear at her heart so it would have made it impossible for her to leave me? She and my father knew what they had to do to get ahead. But that one year, without the security of my own parents, has stayed with me all these years. I hated living in my aunt's house. I missed the doting of my parents, and I was terrified of the outhouse, where I had seen snakes, spiders, and lizards. And I was so bewildered. Nobody would answer my questions, "Where is my mother? Why did she leave me here?"

How could I possibly understand that the decision to leave me with this aunt was inspired by a need to secure a better future for me? My father had crunched the numbers. Though he had little book learning, he always had a very astute business mind. He knew if he and my mother could be free for one year of the demands of parenthood, they could get ahead financially. So they chose a hard path for a year to build us a better life. In their year of working without me around, they were able to move to a larger apartment, in which they occupied two rooms and rented out the others.

I returned to it one day with them from the South, and said very little. A few years later, their work ethic would become my own work ethic, but at the time, their decision only caused me misery. We never talked about that lost year—my parents simply didn't discuss difficult and disturbing incidents. But I was scarred by it, and I was left with such a deep feeling of abandonment that I took it with me for years, all the way into middle age and beyond. And I still believe that that year—and the fear I subsequently had of being left behind—caused me to stick with men who were absolutely wrong for me later in my life. I also carried with me a feeling that I had done something wrong to deserve such treatment from people I loved so very much.

But that day when my parents finally brought me back to New York, I will say this: a far more comfortable life was beginning for all of us in every way.

My parents were all about moving up. But stylish as Harlem was in those years, it was still a ghetto. So early on, my father talked of moving to the suburbs—and Mother urged him along with the idea. He once interrupted a game of stickball outside our home to have the children who were playing take their coats off his car—he prided himself on having a clean car—and when he returned he found his windshield broken. It only reinforced his dream of having a nice lawn on which his little girl could play without worry, and a garage to keep his Chrysler safe from stickball players. It took a long time to move. But he was doing well. By the time I was in kindergarten, he had saved enough to purchase a brownstone as a rental property. So he became a landlord.

If you tried to tell me we lived in a rough part of town or that we were low on the social totem pole, I would not have believed you. To me, my parents were a king and queen, and I was their princess, a Harlem princess. Though my father rarely said very much, they adored me and surrounded me with everything, from toys and clothes to hugs at night, that made me feel loved and secure, and on a pedestal all my own.

I took my role in my elementary school production of *Pinocchio* very seriously, and so did my mother. "All right, let's study your lines now," she'd tell me. We'd rehearse together. "Did you like that, Mommy?" I'd say, working until my bedtime.

I was relentless in my determination to have every little line and every little action perfected, and she was with me every step of the way, as much a coach as an accomplice. "Should I say it like this or that? Faster or slower? High or low?" For weeks, I couldn't talk about anything but that elementary school play. My mother never tired of it.

And she took my costume as seriously as any mother possibly could. I was only seven years old, and it was only made of crepe paper, but you'd have thought it was wardrobe for a queen the way she fussed over it. "How should I wear this, Mommy? What about the hat?" I played Jiminy Cricket, the little voice of conscience. It was a good role for me, since my parents had been vigilant in teaching me about propriety at every level. The girl who was Carol Diann was not allowed to chew gum or use rough language or hang around on the street after school with other girls on our Harlem block. I had to practice piano, not one hour, but two, every day. "All respectable young people know how to play the piano," my mother would say as I'd sit down and tap the keys on the spinnet in our living room. "Does that make you *not* respectable?" I always wanted to ask her. Just outside the window, kids were playing, hanging around. I never cared about missing out on that. I had my music, a civilizing sound in a scrappy neighborhood.

I had to devote all my extra time to my studies and to rehearsals for the Tiny Tots choir at the Abyssinian Baptist Church. Our church was the most important institution in Harlem, overseen by Adam Clayton Powell Sr., and a place where you dressed to the nines every Sunday. My father was a deacon. I was always dressed better than any other child, and I was a natural talent, never shy or apprehensive in front of the congregation. I loved being the soloist, and to this day I remember stepping out of the line of other little singers in our black-and-white robes, and looking way down beyond the pulpit to my audience, opening my mouth, and with only a little fear, opening it to sing "Balm in Gilead" and "No Hiding Place Down There." The chorus behind me backed me up in a way that felt so empowering. The congregation was smiling in the brightly lit tabernacle, with friendly black faces all around and above me in the balconies, as they fanned themselves in the heat. Afterward, when I took off my robe to go home, or perhaps to a carefully prepared picnic at Edgecombe Park, I looked regal. My mother saw to that. It was always her goal to make me look as clean and pretty as possible.

For piano recitals, she would seize the chance to be my stylist and fixate on putting me in the loveliest dress—organza or cotton with crinolines underneath. Sometimes I'd go with her to buy fabrics at the open market under the bridge of the L train on Park Avenue. "Oh no, no, no, no," she'd say as she tested how quickly a fabric would wrinkle in her hands. If it stayed wrinkled, no matter how pretty, and how much I wanted her to have it made into a dress for me, she'd put it down. Then she'd pick up another fabric and tug at it as the subway rumbled on the tracks above us. It was hot, and she still had to prepare dinner thirty blocks away. But there was no deterring her. "No, not this one, either," she'd say as she'd put down the fabric and move on. It always took a long time to find just the right thing, but even when I was hungry or tired on our shopping expeditions, I was never impatient. I marveled at my mother's resolve, the fact that she knew so much about fabrics, and knew exactly what she'd have the seamstress do with it.

"Gathered here, and with a sash to tie in a bow in the back," she'd say. "We need a Peter Pan collar and pleats down the front, but not too many." Her voice was lusty, her accent more rural Southern than Harlem. At times, she seemed like Sophia Loren.

Sometimes she'd take me to Macy's, and it felt like I was seeing the world with her as my tour guide. When she'd put a yellow bow in my hair, she'd fuss with it until it was just so. "Here, not there," she'd say as her strong fingers fluttered over my head like bees pollinating a flower. "Just off to the side so it doesn't distract too much from your eyes."

She was of the generation that had just come North from the South. And they were obsessed with looking clean and attractively dressed because we lived in a country that promoted the idea that blacks were neither. If you talk about racism, it all began to gel for me when I realized why my mother was so obsessed with cleanliness. Well, she always knew what she wanted. I guess she was like her mother in that way. My grandmother Rebecca was quite sharp, a formidable person. She was also incredibly proper, a hardworking country woman who ran a cotton and tobacco farm. She saw to it that my mother was educated, the first girl in her North Carolina town to be sent off to high school the next town over—a very big deal in the early twentieth century. I don't think there were many women who would actually run their own businesses at the time, and certainly not many black women. I still remember when I'd stay with her as an older child during my summer vacations, and going to town and observing how she conducted herself. The South was not like the North in the 1940s. When we went shopping, I remember hating the way white men did business with my grandmother, when she was selling them hogs or chickens. Instead of Rebecca, they called her Becky, and spoke to her as if she was a child. But she would not respond, she just stood her ground until her business was done. I learned something from her quiet dignity in the presence of racism. "Thank you, Mr. Smith," she'd say, without any tone of annoyance in her voice. "I'll see you next week." It was difficult to watch, in one way, but impressive in another. Studied composure helped her get along in her world. It wasn't easy being a woman running a farm. But my grandfather, who died when he stepped on an electrical wire, had left her his business and she had to run it with an iron hand, employing local blacks and treating them no better or worse than her white counterparts did. She would have them picked up for work each day in a mule-drawn wagon, rather than a truck. That's how long ago it was. And when her workers lined up to get their pay at the end of the day, they had their cotton bags full on their shoulders, and she weighed them very carefully to determine exactly what they were to be paid. Once she decided, there was no arguing with Miz Rebecca, as they called her. She was a fair boss, but tough. And she would not allow me in the fields to work, absolutely not.

I spent many happy summers on the porch of her big

house, listening to the crickets and honeybees, looking out at all the children who were working, and hearing the screen door slam as the family came and went from the kitchen. I had to dress every morning and, after breakfast, sit on that porch in an ironed cotton dress, ramrod straight, with hands folded politely. It was hot in all those clothes, but my mother and grandmother were far too formal to consider changing the way a child should dress merely for comfort.

There was only one day my grandmother let me pick cotton, and only because I asked.

I walked out into the field with the others, who were smiling at me, the special child finally on the ground among them. "Well, look who it is," one boy said. "Gonna make a dollar today, Miss Johnson?" I nodded. I had my burlap bag, and for once, I wasn't in a stiff starched dress. It felt liberating in a way, but also completely alien to be in overalls. I bent down to pick my first boll. It made my fingers bleed. I knew cotton did that, but didn't think it would happen to me. You couldn't get blood on the cotton you put in your bag, and I didn't know when I would stop bleeding. So I quit after picking about fifteen cents' worth. I just wasn't meant for the fields, not at all.

"Oh, it's fun to be on the porch," I'd say when asked how I was doing.

Just like in Harlem, I was aware of the fact that I was separated from other children. I was Miss Rebecca's granddaughter, privileged and special. Both she and my mother made that clear. I once rode on a bus "down South" that was full of children, and they all stopped speaking when they saw me. They stared at me because I was the dressed-up girl from New York. It made me feel awkward, but good, too. My mother and grandmother wanted me to project a "better than" quality. And I did, but with that came a feeling of "separated from" that has stayed with me my whole life.

I always felt I was on display. At night my thick hair, after being curled, was wrapped in brown paper so I would have Shirley Temple curls in the morning. What was a black girl doing with Shirley Temple curls anyway? Well, Shirley Temple was the biggest star in the world when I was little, universally adored. So why shouldn't I look like her? It didn't occur to me that we were different because of race. My elementary school was integrated, with Jewish, Italian, Hispanic, and black children. It wasn't until junior high school that the kids took offense at my formal way of dressing. To some extent, I was a snob. That's what my parents wanted me to be. "Carol Diann," my mother would croon as she fawned over me, "let's try to do better than that!" Across the street from our brownstone, people spilled out of an apartment building at all hours of the night. Children hung out on the corners and played loud games of tag, which my mother forbade me from joining. "Such a waste of time," she'd say. Homework was to be done right away, piano lessons at Mrs. Carmen Shepherd's Music School on Convent Avenue were relentless for eight years. Learning music was valued among the strivers of our community, and even in the poorer homes, you'd find a piano among the furniture.

Hard as we worked, my mother (who helped my father manage his rental property when he was working as a subway conductor) found time for the kind of fun she thought would enrich me. Sometimes, on weekends, we'd take a break to see a puppet show or circus, or even take in a Broadway play from balcony seats. A high point was seeing Ethel Merman in *Annie Get Your Gun*. Her voice and confidence onstage were just awe-inspiring. I reveled in the spectacle. The heavy burgundy curtains hung in an ornate and gilded theater full of well-dressed white people. The lights went down and a spotlight would hit the orchestra leader in the pit. My heart swelled with the music. And when the curtains rose on sets so elaborate they took my breath away, it was hard to believe that the performers were real. But they were. Even if they weren't in shows with elaborate costumes, I marveled at how an actress could just take the stage, open her mouth, and, without so much as a microphone, fill a theater with a song. I was lucky that my mother liked attending the theater so much. She made me feel at home there. Maybe too much at home. One time, she took me to see *The Voice of the Turtle,* which she assumed from the title would be a light, funny children's show. In actuality, John Van Druten's play was very adult, and included scenes of a black serviceman on leave employing prostitutes. Instead of pulling me out, Mother watched with me and, when it was over, told me, "Let's not mention this to your father." I have to laugh at this memory today because the prudish views she maintained her whole life—sex was not to be discussed ever—were always an issue for me.

My father, meanwhile, was a man of such propriety that he even objected to the delicate amount of makeup that my mother wore to church.

"It doesn't look respectable, Mabel," he'd say.

"Oh, John, what do you know?" My mother would laugh.

My own propriety made me a target in my young teenage years. "What is wrong with you, Johnson?" the kids in school asked. It wasn't just my curls: it was the whole package. I didn't smoke, wore oxfords and bobby socks (instead of heels with long socks stretched up to the knee and secured with rubber bands) and I never hung out on the street. I carried myself in the ladylike way my mother taught me, and I only associated with children she and my father deemed socially acceptable, such as Sylvia O'Gilvie, who lived nearby and came from a home (a brownstone) with two respectable parents and a car. Of course a mother like Sylvia's had her own heightened sense of social hierarchy that was even more finely developed than my mother's. One day when I came to visit, Sylvia's mother told me Sylvia was out playing with her "real friends." Somehow it became clear that that meant children whose parents were from the West Indies, not the South, and who had lighter skin and straighter hair than mine. My mother encouraged me not to be hurt, but rather to pay no attention to such unkindness.

When Mom saw that a scholarship program was being offered through the Metropolitan Opera, she saw to it that I applied for it and enrolled at the age of ten. Each week she took me to lessons, where I learned to use my diaphragm to support my vocal cords. I learned about breathing, pulling down the tailbone, and all kinds of things about how the body works when it performs. It was overwhelming and all-consuming work, and I threw myself into it, delighted to know adults cared enough about me to want me to perform at my best level.

Meanwhile, I prevailed as a little princess in public school. And it was enough to drive my classmates to some vicious acts of cruelty. One time, a gang of girls followed me all the way home, trying to beat me up and rip out my curls. My mother was shocked to find me arriving at our front steps out of breath and disheveled. "You girls go home now," she called through our barred ground-floor window. "Leave us alone." They thrust their hands through our window and tried to grab her and they didn't leave until my mother called the police. It had never occurred to her that thirteen-year-old girls could threaten us on our own property. The next day at school, the bullying started again as we were filing up the stairs. I made it to the landing before a wave of bodies knocked me down. When the girls pulled my curls, my head hit the floor. I fought back, kicking, punching, and scratching with all my strength, and when they stopped, I was bruised and large clumps of hair had been torn out of my head. Not long after that, a guidance counselor named Mrs. Humphreys, whom I will always revere for her wisdom, recommended I apply to the High School of Music and Art. It was located nearby. But it was an entirely new world.

I refused to go. Although I didn't have a lot of friends at school, I didn't want to leave behind the few I had. But my mother, like that wonderful guidance counselor, saw the opportunity. While my father had to be reassured that this would pave my way to acceptance at the revered Howard University, a place I'd heard about for years as the most prestigious black university in the nation, my mother knew that a high school for the arts would improve me in all kinds of ways, just as she knew the right clothes would broadcast to the world the kind of person I was. I can't say her instincts did anything but serve me well and push me up the social ladder she and my father found so daunting.

I auditioned for Music and Art by playing piano and singing two songs. All my training as a Tiny Tot at church and with the Metropolitan Opera's scholarship program for children paid off. I got in and found, to my absolute joy, teachers talking to students as if they were adults and students engaged in work at intellectual levels I had never seen before in my life. The school was a hotbed of creativity, one of the two schools that inspired the movie *Fame* years later. But you needed to apply yourself as a thinker, not just a performer. To that end, the school seemed to know no limits. Eleanor Roosevelt even came to our auditorium for a three-hour forum. Eugene Ormandy, the conductor of the Philadelphia Symphony Orchestra, came to perform. We watched him, a little man, tap with his baton and speak so quietly to our student musicians that it was a real lesson in the power of keeping your voice down. I was thrown into thinking about music theory and all kinds of things I'd never thought about before. What was American music and where did it come from and why? Where were Gershwin's origins? What about Duke Ellington? They took your brain at that school and really stretched it. Even your activities on weekends had to be accounted for. "Miss Johnson," one teacher said, "what newspapers do your parents read at home?" When I told him which tabloids we had around the house, he insisted I buy the Sunday *New York Times* instead, and that I report to him on articles I'd read. This was really the beginning of a new life of the mind for me. I had to read the *Atlantic Monthly,* too. At first it was difficult, with so much to understand. But eventually I started to see how reading the *Times* and serious journalists could give me a broad picture of a fascinating world, all told in an erudite manner. Reading, I suddenly realized, could be so much more enlightening than I'd ever known.

It didn't take long for me to feel I was outgrowing my parents, even my mother, who had gone to such trouble to instill her taste and her values in my young soul.

This uncomfortable feeling of becoming more worldly than your own parents isn't uncommon among daughters of any generation. But it is something that was hard to reconcile with my earlier life, and it would temper the deep bond I had with my mother in our years ahead.

But to their great credit, as I thrived in my first years at a great high school, John and Mabel Johnson continued to pursue a better life. They had property, tenants, and two sources of income. My father learned that it was wise to trade in his car every two years for a newer model. And while I was taking my work at the High School of Music and Art very seriously, in both performing and academics, my parents spent the mid-1940s realizing their dream of finally moving to the suburbs—to Yonkers, just north of the city. At first, my father had been looking for a house. But when realtors showed only inferior places down by the railroad tracks, he decided to build his own. He got a tip from a friend about a lot on Dunston

Avenue in a nonintegrated area. "Just look," the friend warned. "Don't stop, don't talk to anybody." Heaven forbid the white neighbors would think that a black man might want to move in his family. In some ways, it was the same scenario Lorraine Hansberry wrote about fifteen years later in *A Raisin in the Sun*. But Dad bought the lot, found a contractor, and started building. Shortly after, someone, perhaps the KKK, stepped in and building supplies stopped arriving at the site. Then the contractor disappeared. Now, these days we have contractors disappear on us for all kinds of reasons. This was very different, and it took fortitude to overcome. But eventually, the house was finished and my father moved us in—me, my mother, and my brand-new baby sister, Lydia. He kept shotguns in the closet, "just in case," he'd say.

I didn't pay any attention. If I had not been so preoccupied with my music and learning lines for my high school's sophisticated productions, going to see MGM musicals whenever I could, and then reading about singers and actors in magazines, perhaps I would have heard my parents discussing how someone drove by early one morning and fired shots through our front window. I would have heard about how the local police came to investigate the incident, but—no surprise—found no leads and never followed up. I would have heard about how someone from the neighborhood piled kindling alongside our home and set it on fire. Fortunately, the facade of our house was brick, hard as our determination.

And just as luckily, most of the movies those days were of an escapist nature that kept my anxiety level low. I considered myself, from a young age, a movie connoisseur. Though I was upset that, except for the occasional character actor, these films were devoid of anyone but white actors, I saw almost everything. I took it all in. I saw Vivien Leigh in *Gone With the Wind,* and like many black girls of my era, I wanted to be Scarlett O'Hara. And although that was impossible, I knew when I saw her performance, which displayed the same composure and manners my mother had been trying to teach me my whole life, that I could also be an actress.

The one black female performer in those days who truly inspired me was Lena Horne. I was thirteen when I first saw her in *Words and Music,* the 1948 MGM musical based on the partnership of Richard Rodgers and Lorenz Hart. Lena had a "guest appearance." This was Hollywood's way of featuring black performers in white movies but not weaving them into plotlines so that their scenes could be cut from versions distributed in the South. It made me happy to know she was out there, and there was nobody else like her on-screen or onstage at the time. She just overwhelmed everyone with her beauty in a way that made race less relevant. Beauty and talent, it seemed, allowed race barriers to be relaxed.

I have to laugh at how my mother went out of her way to keep me from seeing Lena on film. I'm not sure if she didn't want me to compare myself to her or think that I didn't have a chance, because there was only room for one genteel black actress. Later, as my singing began to draw reviews and critics began to call me the second Lena Horne, I told them that I preferred to be known as the first Diahann Carroll. That came from my mother, who had nurtured me to believe that all things were indeed possible.

But that's getting ahead of the story. When I was a young teen, the only person comparing me to anyone on the big screen (other than my mother of course!) was me. I took in all kinds of movies and held them close to my heart—dramas, comedies, and, of course, musicals. And I carefully studied the performances in them, taking in every detail, from costumes to gesture, diction, and the impeccable timing of dialogue. My father found this level of interest a bit intense. "You need to focus on your textbooks," he said. "You're going to college, not Hollywood." But Mother was more complicit with my ambitions. She would always take the time, when she had it, to discuss the films we'd seen together.

We were as close as any mother and daughter could be, but I wasn't long for the racist troubles of Yonkers or a long commute to school in Harlem. To be able to maintain matriculation at the High School of Music and Art, I established residence with a single aunt in Manhattan. And every day in that school—full of the kind of intellectual curiosity and ambition I had never seen in classrooms before—I thrived. It made me question my mother's insulation, and wonder if I couldn't open her up to the world I was now reading about in Sunday's *New York Times*. But she was too busy to pay much attention to the needs of an adolescent with worldly pretensions. "Reading the *New York Times* is your assignment, not mine," she'd tell me. She had to decorate her new house in Westchester and care for a second child. She filled her days with shopping for furniture and making her new home as impeccable as possible.

I filled my days with studying, music, and performing.

One day, a friend in the city took a picture of me posing in my sister's baby carriage and sent it to a fashion editor at *Ebony* magazine, one of the few national publications devoted to showing blacks at their best. I didn't look anything like the sophisticated models in the magazine, but to my surprise, six months later, *Ebony* responded with a letter. Much as I spent my life shopping with my mother, who adored clothes, neither of us actually knew the first thing about fashion. That much was clear when I dressed myself for a midtown Manhattan morning interview at Johnson Publications (*Ebony, Jet,* and *Sepia* were their magazines) in a gray taffeta cocktail dress that would only have been appropriate for evening. To make matters worse, I wore a lavender straw hat with a veil and matching lavender gloves. And instead of something as simple as stockings, I oiled my legs so they wouldn't look too ashy.

The fashion editor of *Ebony* opened the door to find, not the pretty young lady from the photographs, but a living example of how not to dress for a meeting. She must have been able to see past the lurid outfit to the high cheekbones, tall, slim figure, and sincere innocence of the little lady I actually was trained to be. So she hired me, and sent me off to a hairdresser who warned me to pay attention to all the makeup artists I'd meet before going in front of photographers. Right away I learned to carry a leather hatbox, containing black pumps, black and white gloves in various lengths, and my own makeup. I learned the difference between daywear and nightwear. I was getting a whole new education, one that my mother, I was intrigued to find, could not provide for me.

To further me along, someone at Johnson Publications recommended I enroll at Ophelia DeVore's Charm School in Harlem. One day I walked up a staircase just inside a door on a bustling 125th Street to find a tall, imposing woman with a stern but kindly look in her eye. I loved Ophelia DeVore and her stylish staff of strong-minded women at first sight. Mrs. DeVore was very charming, well dressed, and committed to teaching us how to carry ourselves properly as young ladies who hoped to have careers in modeling and onstage. She instructed with a kind of caring gentility. She knew we were from underprivileged backgrounds and we didn't have the money or sophistication to have been raised to understand the finer things in life, including social graces and posture. "You must tuck under, and keep the shoulders straight," she'd tell me if my behind was not aligned with my head. Unlike today, when sex seems to inform every step, girls were chastised in class for the slightest flirtatious movement. "You're walking too seductively, and that's not the way to get work as a model," we were told. To pay for class, I became a part-time receptionist. I'd sit outside Mrs. DeVore's large studio, lined with mirrors, and inhale the mannerly ambience she had created.

My first job for Johnson Publications was to pose with a few other teenagers in petticoats. Imagine how my father responded to that! There I was in a magazine read by his community, posing only in a bra and petticoat, and he was so upset I had to agree never to pose in those kinds of shots again. I was far too young at the time to tell him he was in danger of being a hypocrite. Much as he liked to promote only the most upright behavior, he was taking the flirting in our church just a little too far. Well, that church, after all, was full of women terribly excited to be under the same roof as the stunningly handsome Adam Clayton Powell Sr. And any handsome male whom women there would see (and especially one in black tie and white gloves serving as a deacon, like my father) turned their well-pressed and -curled heads. It's only recently that I have come to realize that a church where everyone is looking his or her best can also become something of a henhouse, and maybe even a brothel. At any rate, my father had been unfaithful for years. I still remember the time he took me with him to visit the home of one of his female "friends." She lived on St. Nicholas Avenue, not far from us, in a well-appointed apartment. Even at the age of seven, I knew something was not proper when she greeted us at her door in a flowing peignoir. Prim and proper in my patent-leather shoes and sky-blue smock dress as innocent as anything Shirley Temple was wearing, I sat down in her small front parlor. It was stuffy. A clock on the mantel was ticking, making me feel like a bomb about to explode. They chatted for a while, and the woman said some pleasant things to me about my church singing. But I knew being with her was terribly wrong even then. By osmosis, I had learned from my parents what was and wasn't proper. I was ashamed for all of us.

And so, in my mind, the strict churchgoing father with family values had no real grounds for objecting to my posing in petticoats in a magazine. But I agreed that I had done something wrong in order to placate him. Soon enough, people from the neighborhood and at church found me posing in that spread, and congratulated him. I think he was surprised at how impressed they all were. But then, I was soon getting paid ten dollars an hour, an impressive sum in those days that went right into my college account. It was hard for my father to put up much of an argument. I was succeeding, even before college, in a way that my driven, disciplined parents had never expected.

The more I modeled for Johnson Publications, the more I supplemented what I was learning at the High School of Music and Art. Innocent as I was, I was getting a chance to see the unimaginably cosmopolitan worlds of successful black editors and publishers, who had secretaries and expense accounts. It was the 1950s in New York City, and seeing a woman like Freda DeKnight, the fashion editor of *Ebony,* riding in a limousine to a photo shoot on Sutton Place left a deep impression, to say the least. I knew I had my mother to thank for preparing me for all this, and pushing me off the cliff, as it were, to take on the life of a model and a performer, but I never thanked her.

My success was thanks enough for her in those days.

I had a friend in high school named Elissa Oppenheim. She was a piano player and I was a singer. We'd practice together at each other's home and worked on an act that we were sure would break us into show business. She was the one who wrote to *Arthur Godfrey's Talent Scouts* for an audition. It was a very popular television show in the early 1950s. When we got our audition, the name of our act, Oppenheim and Johnson, was deemed too imposing, according to a sharp-tongued producer who met with us. At the time I didn't see the point. But it is a bit of a mouthful, I suppose, for a couple of teenage girls with a high sincerity level. So Elissa changed her name to

Lisa Collins, and for me she suggested Diahann Carroll. It turned out my first name was spelled that way on my birth certificate anyway, as I soon found out when applying for a job at Macy's.

The audition was nerve-racking, as freckle-faced Elissa banged her heart out on a grand piano on an overlit stage. I forgot about the serious-looking people scrutinizing us, plunged into my song, "Tenderly," and gave it all I had. Afterward, we waited in the lobby for a verdict. A producer came out to tell us the singer was wanted, but not the pianist.

I told Elissa that I didn't want to do it without her. She told me I had to.

I won first prize on the television show, and went in to see Mr. Godfrey to discuss appearing on his daily radio show. This time, it was with my mother. She was looking unusually beautiful that day, in a formfitting suit and high heels that made her voluptuous body all the more seductive, and Mr. Godfrey, a man fully in touch with his power over us, flirted with her right under my eyes. Then he told us a racist joke about a slave who fell off a wagon or some silly thing. And Mom laughed. What was going on here? I felt my palms go sweaty with discomfort. How dare this man insult my mother? How dare he insult me like that? It was very confusing to see this woman, my mother, who had such a keenly developed sense of propriety, allow herself to be so complicit with such vulgarity. The sense of correctness (ingrained in me since I was a toddler) went into high alert, and suddenly the power this bullying celebrity had to change my life didn't mean anything to me. I told him, "I don't think my mother appreciates jokes like that." He fell silent and got a look of consternation on his otherwise pleasant bland face that I'll never forget. And my mother? She looked absolutely shocked at my response. All her life, both she and my father, dignified and upright as they were, had had to stoop and bow their heads when faced with racism. They didn't want to make any waves. They wanted to move up in the world, and getting upset about how hateful racism could be was never their approach. After a moment, Mr. Godfrey leaned in to his buzzer and told his secretary, "Miss Smarty Pants here is going to be on our radio show next week." By holding my own, I had prevailed. I wish I could have impressed that point on my mother. But when it came time to appear on my first radio broadcast, he continued flirting with her and she allowed it, even as she became more and more embarrassed. Her discomfort could not stop Arthur Godfrey, a driven entertainer. And you know what? It didn't stop me, either. I returned to the show to sing for the next three weeks, an unqualified success.

Of course my mother found this as exciting as I did. I was, after all, her child, and it was terribly validating for her to see me prevail at such an early age. She'd get up at the crack of dawn with me, dress herself carefully, weigh in on my outfit, then drive me to the studio, where I had to put on my own makeup to perform in front of a live radio audience. It was so exciting to be waiting in the dressing room with well-known singers, such as the McGuire Sisters. And the acclaim we'd get all week from neighbors who heard me on the radio pleased her, of course, but it was the backstage glamour, the entry into an exclusive world my mother had never imagined within her reach, that made her happiest. And she developed a taste for it right away; this intoxicating inside world of show business got into her blood early on. Well, why not? She lacked what it took to crack the code of black society in our community. But suddenly she was on the inside of an even more impressive world. Those early days of accompanying me were our happiest times, as triumphant as they were nerve-racking, really. I was still so young that I needed her to be there with me, and we both knew it. My father did, too. Yes, there was a toddler in the house, but my mother always made sure someone else could look after her.

Sometimes she'd see a handsome man on our rounds. Proper as she could appear to be, she wasn't afraid to let me know when a man had sex appeal.

"Well . . ." She'd sigh. "He could certainly put his shoes under *my* bed."

Sometimes I'd argue with her, and sometimes I'd agree. "Yes, Mother, he's very attractive and he can certainly put his shoes under my bed, too," I'd say. It was a funny little female-bonding thing, that's all, and we'd laugh at each other in delight.

I still remember how excited she was to help me get ready for a singing contest I had entered in Philadelphia as a teenager. "What are you going to wear? Should we have a new dress made or should we go shopping?" It was never so much about what I was going to sing as what I was going to wear. She loved how pretty I could look, and I loved making her happy. She'd drive me to all kinds of contests. We were as excited as kids.

When I graduated the High School of Music and Art, I

told my parents I could not uphold their lifelong dream of attending Howard University. It was too far away, and it would keep me from my lucrative modeling work with Johnson Publications. My career as a student of psychology at NYU didn't last long, either. I'd show up in class carrying my leather hatbox so I could run off to a photo shoot, and my professors saw this preoccupation reflected in my grades. In my freshman year, I entered a television contest called *Chance of a Lifetime,* and was called in. I sang "The Man I Love" and "Someone to Watch Over Me," and won for three weeks in a row. My prize? A staggering three thousand dollars and a week's booking at the famous nightclub and society venue the Latin Quarter.

A seventeen-year-old girl singing in a nightclub is not exactly a parental dream scenario. The Latin Quarter served liquor. The Latin Quarter had showgirls in scanty costumes. It was no place for a performer to bring her mother. And besides, there was no room for her in such a hectic backstage, with performers changing costumes night by night. I learned by watching, as I did at modeling jobs, the strong-willed women around me. The showgirls at the Latin Quarter, for instance, might have dressed like loose women, but they were very focused and meticulous backstage as they prepared themselves for each costume change, and I heard them discussing diet and exercise with the knowledge of true professionals. It was from them that I learned how important it was to take care of my skin, hair, teeth, and physique, along with my voice. And it was from the transsexual Christine Jorgensen, also performing at the club, that I learned to bow. She was a lovely person. I took it all in, just as I had taken in my mother's lessons in childhood.

And frightened as I was, my mother's training served me well as I took to the stage in my grand gown of tulle and my tiara, and told myself, "Here you go, Diahann Carroll," and stepped out, scared but not paralyzed, to sing my heart out into the darkness.

Around that time, my parents got a call from the Lou Walters office. Lou Walters (Barbara Walters's father) owned the Latin Quarter. He also owned a personal management company and he wanted to sign me. He believed I had a big future in the business. So at the same time as I was leaving NYU, a new education began for me. A young manager from the Walters office named Chuck Wood took me under his wing. He quickly became a mentor, taskmaster, and second family to me.

Although the Walters Office made its bread and butter booking singers into nightclubs and Catskills hotels, Chuck loved the theater. He thought I belonged on Broadway and he was relentless in getting me to sing each song perfectly. "You're stiff," he'd say. "Relax! You're not letting us hear the lyrics! Do it again!" He'd cook dinner for me in his apartment in Greenwich Village, and introduced me to new foods as we continued lessons by his fireplace. He told me to read the work of the playwrights Eugene O'Neill and Arthur Miller. He told me to always remember I had an innate ladylike quality and that I was all about style and class. He didn't want me in tight gowns, and wanted me to retain my soft vulnerability rather than pursue the more obvious raw emotions and sexuality of other singers. He'd advise me to cross my legs more quickly when sitting down and suggest I rid myself of the rhinestones and sequins my mother preferred.

"Remember, you're a lady!" he'd say. "If it ain't real, don't wear it," he chuckled.

My vocal coach, Margo Rebeil, was equally intent and giving. After our lessons, she'd teach me about serving tea. She'd take me for drives in her Packard convertible, and at a cocktail party, she decided it was time for me to try my first glass of champagne.

"You look so pretty tonight," she told me.

If only she knew how much she and Chuck Wood both sounded like my mother. There were times when I ached for Mabel Johnson to be a part of this new life with me. After all, we were buddies, so in love with each other in my childhood that every once in a while, and despite her insistence on discipline, she'd let me stay home from school. "It's raining, and you're getting a cold and shouldn't go out today," she might say.

Hard as he tried, Chuck couldn't get me any roles on Broadway. So he started booking me into nightclubs. My earliest memories of the road were harsh ones. There was only enough money for me to travel alone. I'd stay in squalid, tiny rooms, and sing to half-filled little clubs and at bars where people talked over me. I learned how to deal with every kind of audience in places like that. If there were hecklers objecting to me because I was black, I'd simply move to the other side of the stage and finish my set, as required. What mattered to me was that I was learning to be a professional, and that I was earning a living. Soon enough, Chuck was getting me bookings at Catskills hotels. This was in their heyday, when middle-class Jewish families from the city and suburbs would come up to the mountains to relax. That meant golfing, tennis, sitting by a pool, and then dressing to the nines for dinner and a show. Who do you think was my date?

Mother loved every minute of it. We'd drive up on a warm summer Friday afternoon, car full of luggage and the all-important hatbox, of course, and we'd be welcomed by the hotel staff and taken to our room, which was always spacious and comfortable, and we'd unpack our clothes and become two girls in a dorm room. We'd have such a good time. We could order room service or eat with the other artists. Sometimes we were encouraged to eat with the guests. There was never a sense of being "less than" just because I was a performer, and my mother loved seeing that. She also had a habit of stealing ashtrays. "Do you think they'll miss it?" she asked. "Yes, Mother, I do, but take it anyway." When it was time to prepare for the show, I'd go off to my dressing room and she'd be escorted downstairs. Even as I was taking these jobs very seriously (rehearsing for as long as the musicians could stand it before turning to worrying about everything from my outfit to my microphone and lighting) I was glad to show Mom such a good time after everything she had put into me during my childhood.

On our Sundays in the tranquil Catskills, with my show behind me, we'd have breakfast. We were always dressed nicely. But perhaps not quite as nicely as all the church ladies my father would be discreetly flirting with in Harlem in our absence. Well, he was admired and he wanted to return all the compliments. I was glad to have my mother along with me on those Catskills weekends. But by then, I was already a big girl, and it occurred to me that this was more about fun for her than anything else.

This was the start of my mother following me around for her own pleasure, and enjoying it a little too much. And it was the kind of bad judgment on her part, putting show business ahead of home life, that I repeated in my own marriage and motherhood.

In time, I began getting more work in Manhattan. When I started performing at Café Society Downtown in Greenwich Village, I replaced my tulle and my tiara for more formfitting, seductive dresses. I could hardly fill them out and they needed padding, but when I zipped them up, voilà, I was no longer the skinny innocent ingenue Chuck thought I should be. Inside, even then, however, I was still a child. I was still living at home with my parents in Yonkers, after all. And while I was gaining more confidence and an understanding of how a singer works with musicians, I still had little flair for giving off a more casual air onstage.

"Why don't you consider having a glass of wine to relax you a little," my mother coached me as she drove me to work one night. "You're a little stiff onstage."

"Because, Mother," I said, "I don't do that."

To her great credit, she'd drive me downtown to work, park the car in front of the entrance, and sit there, waiting. She didn't want to go inside. In her complicated mind, this woman whom I'd seen have a cocktail or two at home, deemed nightclubs absolutely improper and no place for a lady. So although she was locked outside, I could feel her watching me as I tried to promote a more sensual self onstage to a room full of people enjoying their drinks and wanting more than anything for me to seduce them.

Years later, I realize just how central her presence was for me in my earliest years. She made it so much easier for me to feel secure in front of so many strangers.

Meanwhile, Chuck Wood's hard work as my personal manager was paying off. One day I found myself summoned to audition for my first Broadway show. It was for none other than Harold Arlen and Truman Capote. The man who wrote "Over the Rainbow" was collaborating with the man who wrote *Breakfast at Tiffany's* on a show set in the West Indies called *House of Flowers*. Chuck thought I'd be perfect for the ingenue's role and had set up an audition, even as the Walters Office was talking to Hollywood about having me try out for a role in an all-black-cast film version of *Carmen* called *Carmen Jones*. But Broadway, to Chuck, was the be-all and end-all. So one day I walked onto the stage of the Alvin Theater and performed to a row of faces in the shadows. One of them was Peter Brook, the English director, who ordered me around in a crisp accent. The other was Capote himself, whose high-pitched Southern drawl was unmistakable. Then there was the gentle voice of Mr. Arlen, a hero of mine, as he was and still is to so many serious singers. I gave it my all for them, and must have done something right because I was called back. But this time, at the callback, a shy casting director in the audience named Monte Kay seemed sure I wouldn't be right for the ingenue role.

The meeting ended, and Harold Arlen himself walked me to the elevator.

"I hear you might be going to California," he said in his gentle voice.

"Yes, I think that's possible," I replied.

"Well, I think it'll be good for you," he continued. "Go,

have a ball, meet new people, and try to live a little!" He was too much of a gentleman to tell me I was too innocent and stiff, even to play an ingenue. I only understood that years later. It was not unlike what my mother had been trying to tell me when she suggested I have a glass of wine to relax before going onstage. I was too stiff, too correct, too fixated on the work—the technique of singing and working with musicians—to have fun and explore any feelings.

The same problem followed me to Hollywood. As did my mother.

Carmen Jones was, as I said, an all-black version of Bizet's *Carmen,* reset in the American South with new lyrics and an unsettling amount of clichéd Southern dialogue. Otto Preminger, the director, had auditioned me for the lead but had cast the beautiful Dorothy Dandridge instead. At the audition, he made me do a scene with James Edwards, a famous actor at the time, in which he was told to paint my toenails. There was no way, at age nineteen, that I was prepared to handle such overt sexuality. Yes, I had a boyfriend back in New York by then, and we had consummated our relationship during an evening I faced with trepidation. But this was beyond my acting abilities. James Edwards, a terribly worldly and seductive man, tried to make me comfortable as we read our lines. But when he finished applying the polish, and blowing on my toes, I had to fight back the nervous giggles of a child. This was not the kind of silly innocence anyone expected from a trained New York performer.

"You! Where are you from?" Mr. Preminger asked.

I froze with fear, then told him.

"And how old are you?"

Sounding more child than woman, I answered, "Nineteen."

"And whoever told you that you were sexy?"

"No one," I shot back.

Then the bullying, all-powerful director threw back his head and laughed.

Dorothy Dandridge got the lead role, and was later nominated for an Academy Award for her performance. Me? I got the role of one of Carmen's sidekicks. It was a small part, but my first big Hollywood break.

It was exciting, in some ways, and discouraging in others. I wasn't too fond of the vulgar, bright red, fringed dress I had to wear with big hoop gypsy earrings. And I especially didn't appreciate a script full of "dees, dems, and dats" to make us sound intentionally down market. The cast, including Pearl Bailey and Harry Belafonte, was superb, and I was delighted to be the young one working with them, just as I loved sitting quietly by Otto Preminger and watching him direct. I was always trying to learn. But it also became quite clear that we were the only blacks on the Paramount lot. It was only temporarily for this "black movie" (there was usually one every few years) that our presence in Hollywood was wanted. We all knew there'd be little place for us after the movie wrapped. Everyone on staff was polite, but thought of us as outsiders.

But you know who was thrilled about everything, start to finish? My mother.

Although I never said I needed her with me, she flew out to Los Angeles to be my chaperone during the shoot. The cast was staying at a little hotel, the Chateau Marmont on Sunset Boulevard. I made sure that my mother was not across the hall, but rather at the other end of the building, passing the time with a friend. They played cards. They had some cocktails, and would go out to lunch or dinner. I was fully aware that she had no reason to be there. My father and sister were home in Yonkers. She did not need to chaperone me, and she was of no use helping me memorize lines or negotiate the business. I could do that with other actors. I was so swamped most days I could barely find the mental energy to check in with her for ten minutes. But I did. "How was your day? What did you do?" I'd ask. She never did much of anything. I felt guilty about that, just as I felt guilty for not inviting her to the set. I knew she hoped to visit. But professionals don't do that. Or maybe the truth is that when you're a novice, you don't want to draw attention to your youth by showing up with your mother. The one time I asked her out to join me for a business dinner, it just felt completely awkward and uncomfortable.

My mother, I'm afraid, was now loving my life far too much.

I certainly got a deep, delicious early taste of Hollywood while in *Carmen Jones*. Sammy Davis Jr., who was becoming a star at the time, had a suite in our hotel, and invited me around all the time. One night, while we were on location in Stockton, California, he asked me to join a group for dinner in a local restaurant. I appeared in my typical formal elegance in a black cocktail dress and white gloves. Sammy gently escorted me to a corner. "You look lovely as always," he told me quietly. "But I think you better remove the gloves, Diahann. We're in Stockton,

not Paris!" He invited me to a party in his suite in West Hollywood another night. There, he introduced me to the painfully
shy Marlon Brando. The next night, a friend of Sammy's asked
me to join them for dinner. Marlon was accompanied by his
girlfriend, and she was dressed in something so blatantly re-
vealing that I became embarrassed and could hardly speak all
evening. Worse, I could not get my mother out of my mind. I
was sure this woman with Marlon was loose, and I couldn't
help imagining Mom walking through the restaurant door, seeing her, and telling me, "I don't think you should be having
dinner with someone like that!" Nor would she have approved
when, on the way out of the restaurant, Marlon gave me a little
pat on the behind. I slapped his face and told him off. My
mother had spoken through me!

It was not something I would have shared with her, though.
We didn't discuss those sorts of things. Nor did I let her know
how ill at ease I was seeing her enjoying being away from home
for so long. Long before the posses of rappers and HBO's
Entourage, she was playing the game. For many weeks, she and
her friend, my aunt Babe, were pretty much on their own in my
hotel. Eventually, they made some friends—my manager, for
one, and others—who would take them to dinner.

My whole life, people who met her were always charmed.

"We love your mother," they'd tell me.

"That's because she isn't your mother," I'd think to myself.

As weeks turned to months on that shoot, I grew more
impatient with her. I had to live on a daily basis with the hole
she was creating in our family. At some point, I must have fig-

ured out that she was avoiding marital problems with my father. She was being independent in some convoluted way, and even trying to be worldly by eschewing domestic life. If only I had spoken up to her about how neglectful she was to my father and sister, who was only five at the time. But what would I have said?

Mom, we need to talk. This isn't just a weekend in the Catskills. You've been away from your home for a very long time. I love you dearly, and you know how grateful I am for your support. I also know you're having a fabulous time out here, and that you're pleased to see how well things have turned out for me. But, Mom, you really need to go home now. I'm old enough to handle things. The only big problem now is you.

Of course I never would have said anything like that. Propriety, as always, got in the way. It always did in my family. Neither of my parents ever spoke about what they were really feeling. My father, an attractive man with every temptation back home, always saw my mother as the great love of his life. He never told her that. And clearly she had issues with sex and sexuality, many of which she managed to pass on to me. How else to explain all the failed marriages and engagements I racked up in years to come? Perhaps my parents had become bored with each other, and had no idea how to have the kind of conversation that might help remedy their sex life. It was, after all, still the 1950s. They didn't read *The Kinsey Report*. What was to be said? And a proud man like my father, who was crippled by his own dignity, was not going to be able to beg his beloved wife to come home. If he did suggest it discreetly, she didn't listen.

It upset me. But it took decades before I could voice my feelings to her.

In the early 1980s, my father finally left my mother, and she fell apart completely. Once again, I heard the news from a family friend. She wasn't sleeping. She wasn't bathing or taking care of herself at all. I was doing two shows a night in Vegas at the time (this was before I received the call for *Dynasty*). I simply could not walk out of my contract to go comfort her, and my little sister, Lydia, in boarding school at the time, was useless to her in such situations. So I called my mother and invited her to stay with me. I didn't want her around while I was working. But I also didn't want her anyplace else.

"Diahann has sent for me," she said to my father. Those were always the magic words. "Diahann has sent for me!" She arrived in Las Vegas, looking composed and attractive. Back in the lotusland of an overpriced hotel, her misery subsided.

Vegas, to my mother, was as good as a sanitarium, with the lulling sound of slot machines and all that eating.

Indeed, over the years, she had become overweight. It was something my father, who ate carefully and exercised all his life, had warned her about. She took care about her dress and carried herself with grace, but weight gain was one of many things in the marriage that she had taken for granted. At any rate, I saw from the moment she arrived that she'd be lifted by her visit. And, as usual, we did not discuss the elephant in the room, the separation. "I'm happy you're here, Mom," I said as she quietly unpacked in her suite.

"Yes; me, too," she said.

"How was the flight?"

"Oh, fine, it was just fine," she said.

This was about all we were capable of saying at that moment. Perhaps I told her I was sorry she was having a hard time and that soon we might want to talk about her plans. But we never had the discussion we should have had about what had happened to her marriage.

The only thing she was able to express was that my father was the one who had done wrong, not her. She claimed to have been mistreated. Even then I knew that this wasn't completely true, and I should have quietly said so. But again, I just didn't know how.

Well, I was a bit busy, with two shows a night for hundreds of people. One of the showstoppers I was doing at the time was "Going Out of My Head." And that kind of summed up my situation. My third marriage had only recently combusted (more on that later), my daughter was estranged from me because she thought I cared more about my career than her (more on that later, too!). Meanwhile, I was completely unsure as to where my career was going, post-*Julia*, but it wasn't looking good. And now here was my mother, devastated to be separated from her husband of thirty-seven years, and right back in the middle of my life, which she had clearly always preferred to her own.

I had a large staff at the time, managers, musicians, personal assistants, and they all adored her and treated her like a queen while I worked like a dog. When the engagement ended, I invited her to live with me in Beverly Hills.

Thus began the last act of my mother's life, a new beginning for us in Los Angeles, a chance to finally have the conversations I had buried for so many years.

In fact, there was nobody whom I learned to speak more freely with than my mother in her last years. That's because I believed in her. Maybe other daughters would have left her to her own ideas. I could not, especially when it came to what she would say about my father. Because he was the one who left the marriage to later remarry, she had convinced herself that she was the one who had been wronged. She played the martyr very well. And she often said disparaging things about my father to my daughter. One night, a few years after my parents' divorce, I was having lunch at my mother's place in the Valley in Sherman Oaks. We bought that house and I hired my decorator to gut and reconfigure it for her needs. She adored it, a sweet little ranch house with lovely landscaping, perfect for lunch with her church-lady friends.

We were in her sunny kitchen at the breakfast nook, and she was telling me she had spoken to some friends in New York who told her my father had remarried. And I don't know where she got this particular piece of information, but she decided to share with me that this woman and my father were having oral sex. She was disgusted at the idea of a woman who would do such a thing and felt my father was sinning horribly.

Before I could stop myself, I blurted out, "Well, thank God Dad has found a real sexual partner!" She squirmed in her seat.

"Diahann," she said. "What in the world are you saying? I cannot believe you would condone such indecent and sinful behavior."

"Mother, sexuality is a glorious part of the human experience, not something to be ashamed of. I know you have tried to teach me all my life that this creates sin, original sin. Do you understand how your kind of attitude has impacted my life? There is *pleasure* in sex, Mother. And you refused to teach me about it, which is enough to drive any man away."

Perhaps it was a bit much, a bit theatrical, but at that point, I was looking at four failed marriages in my own life along with two broken engagements. So I was frustrated with both her and my own romantic history. She was in her eighties and I was in my sixties. Both of us were past our primes, yet the intensity of this conversation was the kind that belonged to youth, not old age.

Many of my friends who adored her for being my sweet little mother were angry with me when she told them about my blunt conversations. They were ready to kill me because they couldn't even say these kinds of things to themselves, much less to their mothers. But looking at it now, I'm glad I tried. We trusted each other.

In those last years, we started to have more fun together than ever before. It was almost like our early days in New York, when she could do no wrong. I look at scrapbooks of photographs from my later years as a young senior citizen and find her in every other shot in her tinted glasses. There she is in one shot with Lenny Kravitz. There she is with Roscoe Lee Browne. There she is with Joan Collins. She's like the Forrest Gump of my life. And looking back now, I'm so glad she could enjoy it.

I just loved that we became pals again in her last years. We went shopping at malls in the Valley, and we'd eat dreadful Nedick's hot dogs just like we did on Thirty-fourth Street when she took me to Macy's in my childhood. Only instead of her giving me fashion advice, I was giving it to her. By then I had been on the International Best Dressed list. I was a senior style paragon who understood understatement, the pleasures of minimalism, beige, and black. My mother had a different approach, which I'd have to call "haute carnivale." When it came to accessorizing, more to her was more. And if you have some sparkle on the sweater, why not have a little on the belt and skirt, too?

"Mother, please," I'd say when she'd get in my car to go to lunch. "I look at you and I don't know if I'm coming or going. We cannot wear the beads, big earrings, necklace, and scarf all at the same time. It's too much. Really! Something has to go!"

"Diahann," she'd say as she adjusted those tinted glasses, "I look fine."

I remembered hearing the advice years ago to always remove one thing before leaving the house, and tried to explain it to her. It went right over her head.

"Just take off the earrings, Mom. Please!"

She just laughed and shook her head. "You know, Diahann, every time you approve of someone's attire, she's dressed as if she's going to a funeral."

She was right. I, who had been dressed exuberantly in the day by Arnold Scaasi and Bill Blass, had become seriously sedate in my latter years. She, on the other hand, was still having a ball with her colorful clothes, like a girl in a sparkly fantasy.

I sat in that car, grinning, even as I shook my head.

"Okay, Mom, I'll make a deal with you. If you take off either the necklace or the earrings or the scarf, then you can decide where we go to lunch today."

She never did. But I let her choose the restaurant anyway.

It happens eventually: the end. I was lucky it took as long as it did.

In her last years, when she was close to ninety, I'd notice crumbs on her clothes and stains on her sleeves, and I had to find a way to tell her without letting her know how badly she was failing. But she wanted to dress and wear heels right to the end, like me.

Eventually, she was in and out of emergency rooms, because she refused to have full-time help around. "I don't want you," she'd tell them. "You're making me old before my time!" It became painfully clear she could not live alone in her house anymore. Against her wishes, our old friend Sylvia and I toured a lovely place near my home in Hollywood. And I did something very clever. I spoke with a young lady working there, and I said to her, "You know, I really have a terrible problem. I want my mother to move here so she'll be safe, but she doesn't know a soul in this building, so I'm very worried." And this young lady smiles at me, and says, "I know who you are. You're Diahann Carroll. You were always so pleasant to everyone when you came to shop at my uncle's antique store, Ferrantes, on Melrose Place in Hollywood. So I'm going to keep an eye on your mother and see that she gets a perfect room over the garden fountain." I was so pleased. And I thought to myself, "So after spending all that money on antiques, it finally paid off!"

When we drove her over to look at the place, she was dressed to the nines, and although unhappy, she did enjoy arriving in my Rolls-Royce, just so people knew where she was coming from. Then I saw the look on her face when she saw how deluxe the place was, or perhaps a better word would be *grand*. Dining room was very nice. TV and game room? Not bad at all. I told her, "Okay, we don't have to speak to anyone today about any of this. Let's just go to the Beverly Wilshire for a fabulous lunch." She pouted all the way through it, still angry about having to move out of her house. But we all worked to make her new room in that rest home as much like her house as possible. And eventually, she started to enjoy dressing for dinner with other well-to-do people in the dining room every night, and I was pleased.

Still, it was sad to see her wane. One day, my dear friend Selbra Hayes asked what did I think would make my mother happiest, and suggested inviting my father out to visit. Immediately, I recognized the importance of that advice. My father was single again. His second wife had passed away several years earlier. So I invited him out to Los Angeles. I told him Mom wanted him to see where she was living.

He arrived, eighty-eight years old, still tall and so handsome. And when I brought those two together, and they saw each other for the first time after so many years, it was the best Hollywood love scene I could imagine. They both looked ecstatic, like there was nowhere else they wanted to be. After a few minutes, we all had to sneak out and allow them to have their time alone together. My father stayed with me all week. And every morning he would get up and dress impeccably. We'd have breakfast. Then I'd drive him over to see Mom and he'd stay there with her all day. Maybe it was my dream as well as theirs, to have them back together, if only for a week. He came back again a year later, when she was still well enough to sit with him outdoors. And they looked like they'd never been apart. I was having my own problems with Vic, my fourth husband, at the time. But seeing my own parents together like that, so happily together—it gave me the kind of hope I never would have expected at that stage of my life.

One night I couldn't sleep and I went to see her. By that point, she was being taken care of by hospice workers because it was near the end. An aide told me she was having difficulty breathing, and I could tell things were pretty bad. So I climbed into bed with her, careful not to disturb the tubes hooked up to her failing body, and I slowly put my arm around her. She felt so frail. Her breathing was labored. I leaned in to her ear, and kept my nose there for a moment, just taking her in. Then I said very softly, "You do know, Mom, that Dad wants to be with you at the end, when you're both gone, don't you? You're the only one." I waited a moment, then I said, "Did you hear that, Mom? Did you hear what I said?" Some moments passed. Her IV machine dripped, and numbers flashed on machines that beeped and whirred. Then I saw her nodding. I felt her head move up and down against my chest. And then, *then* she smiled. It was faint, but it took my breath away. She heard me. She understood. She was still in love.

We sat together for a while. Then I told her I was going

home to bed, and that in the morning I had to make a speech at the Dorothy Chandler Pavilion, and then I'd return to see her in the afternoon. My driver got a call while I was speaking, and he called me with a message to call him. I knew what had happened. I rushed to her. She lay still in her bed, all life gone from her body. The tubes and machines were gone, too. It was the first time I had ever seen a person who was no longer breathing. I rubbed her forehead, and leaned in and said, "Rest now, Mom. You lived a wonderful life."

She wasn't the only one who was well turned out for the funeral. I wore a stylish Carolina Herrera suit for the occasion, and a big dramatic hat she would have loved. I thought of her when I chose it. I know she would have approved. My mother almost always approved of what I wore. Well, for better or worse, she had my full attention. And when I look back on it now, I'm so glad I was there to give her my love and attention, right to the end. You only have one mother in life, after all.

Not long after she died, I formed a habit of speaking aloud to her. It helped me a great deal to say, "What would you do in this situation, Mom?" It still does. I know that sounds strange, given all the doubts I had about her. But when I was fourteen years old, there was nobody who had more to teach me than my mother. And later, even with all my issues, I always kept in my mind that she only wanted what was best for me. I've had some fans in my time, but nobody could make me feel as special as she did.

She was the first person who made me want to reach for the stars.

Sometimes, when I am listening to certain kinds of music,

particularly the kind she raised me to appreciate—Duke Ellington, Nat King Cole, and Billy Eckstine—I turn it up very loud, and I sing for her. And even though I'm not the best dancer, I dance a little, too.

I dance for my first and most devoted audience.

And on many days I wear tinted glasses just the way she did.

But never with big earrings. Please!

David Frost and Diahann Carroll. (Photograph by Ron Galella/WireImage)

THREE

Men, Take One

NORMA DESMOND HAD HER MAD SCENE AT THE TOP of the stairs. I, on the other hand, had mine in a condo at the top of a high-rise in Beverly Hills in 1998. It was evening, and the lights were off and the entire city of Los Angeles was spread out beneath my walls of windows. Directly below me was Sunset Boulevard, a streaming river of car lights. I had just gotten off the phone with Vic Damone, who had left me for another woman months before, after ten years of marriage. Our conversation had been icy cold. When I hung up I felt newly betrayed, angry, and, more than anything else, desperately and terribly alone. I was sitting on the floor in the dark, teetering on the edge of confusion and madness. Very dramatic! What was I going to do with the rest of my life? I had not planned to be facing my senior years alone. How did it happen? And why?

At one time I adored Vic. We had some lovely, romantic moments in our ten years together. How could I not be seduced by a handsome, impeccably dressed man who would call me in the evenings after I had gotten into bed, and softly croon "Let Me Call You Sweetheart," in an old-world Italian accent? When he first approached me in 1981, we were both performing at the Caribe Hilton in San Juan. Late one night, he sent an extravagant meal to my room, unannounced. It was thoughtful, presumptuous, and funny. I paid it little mind.

Upon our next meeting, I found I could not ignore him any longer. We were doing a show for a charity in a hotel in Palm Beach. On the flight down there, my manager, Roy, explained I would be on the bill with Damone, and that he was set as the closing act. That put me in a very competitive mood. One never wants to open for someone else. When I saw him at rehearsal, he said to me, "Hello, Diana!"—mispronouncing my name. I said to my assistant, "See, I told you—nothing upstairs." Then, while I was performing, he stood in the wings to watch me, which was unconventional, to say the least, and somewhere between flattering and unsettling. After the show, Vic's conductor told me Vic would like to come up for a drink. I thought that would be nice. When he arrived in his tuxedo, I don't know what happened to me, but suddenly I saw his appeal, as if for the first time. He was tan, and his face was handsome, with a strong jawline, lovely salt-and-pepper hair, and dark eyes that seem to suggest the possibilities of something more. I was enjoying his company. Maybe it was the jokes he made—humor is often an aphrodisiac for me—but I was suddenly seeing him in a totally different way. Later, when everyone else had gone home, my assistant asked if I wanted her to stay. I found myself telling her no.

We both went up to New York from there, and we had dinner. I had the impression that he was a hardworking professional who had sustained a strong career for a long time, and I had great respect for that. And it was nice to be with someone who was something of a household name. His suits and shirts were bespoke, and I loved seeing his selection of clothing for dinner or a night out. When he first saw my home in Los Angeles, he remarked how elegant it was, and Cancerian that I am, that pleased me tremendously. Watching him cook was every career woman's dream. On Sundays in New York (I still had my apartment there), we'd go to the markets on Broadway, where he would choose ingredients as obsessively as any chef I'd ever seen. Then, arm in arm, we'd go back to my apartment on Riverside Drive, where he would fly into a happy high gear making the most wonderful pasta. Me? I always took pride in setting a really beautiful table. He loved that. We had a ball. Wherever we'd go, we had fun together.

Sometimes, when we toured, things got a little awkward. Clearly he was of a generation of men (Rat Pack in attitude, I'd say) for whom having a girl in every port was standard practice. Well into my fifties by then, a lady who'd been around the block herself more than once, I was wise enough not to worry about Vic's little lothario history.

When we were performing for a week in Vegas, for instance, this woman would come backstage to see Vic every night after the show with two children. They were dressed for the occasion, and I was always very polite when introduced to them, but I didn't quite understand their relationship to Vic, or perhaps I knew I didn't want to. I mean, we were both too old, really, to worry about each other's past. It wasn't necessary.

One day the phone was ringing in the suite I was sharing with Vic, and he and Roy were all worked up.

"You answer it," Vic said.

"Well, what do you want me to say?" Roy asked.

The two of them sounded like mischievous little boys. It was such a commotion that I finally asked them what was going on and if I could be of any assistance. It turned out that the caller was the lady who'd been coming to the dressing room with her children. She was convinced that Vic was their father, and hoped that he still had feelings for her.

The phone rang again. And as it rang I said to Vic and Roy, "I will answer this phone for you and take care of the situation for good. But you really must be sure you want to be rid of this woman, because once I speak with her, she will never call again."

They told me to go ahead and answer the phone. I did and asked who was calling, and what it was about. "It's not something I can discuss with you," the woman said.

"Well, if this has anything to do with you and the children you are bringing backstage to see Vic after our show, I'd like to tell you about something I've done."

"Oh yeah, what's that?" she said.

"Well, I've set up an organization for women like you

called ICVD. That stands for Illegitimate Children of Vic Damone, and I could have some information sent to you about it if you'd like. We always have a lovely dinner for the women and children they believe are Vic's offspring, and it's a wonderful chance to exchange stories and ideas."

Vic and Roy were choking with laughter as they listened. Maybe I was being insensitive. But on the other hand, was it considerate of this woman to come backstage with her children and constantly call a hotel suite she knew we shared?

"You bitch," the woman said to me. Then she slammed down the phone.

And we never heard from her again.

There are other notable memories. Some were even on golf courses.

He was a seven-day-a-week golfer, and he was keen on teaching me to play. One day we were in Palm Springs, his favorite place, where he was purchasing a second home, and he took me to his favorite course. He was in his immaculate golf pants and V-neck sweater and I was in one of those adorable little golfing skirts, and he was standing up against me, intently instructing me how to hit the ball, and telling me how difficult it was. I went ahead and swung and hit that ball right into the hole. So I turned to him and said, "There! Now I've played golf, okay? I did it. It's done. And I will never understand how one can derive such a great deal of satisfaction from putting that little ball in that little hole more than once. Do I become happier if I do it a second time?" The boyish and surprised look on his tan, adorable face was one of such delight that I just wanted to hug him. Later, he kept telling all his friends what happened, and he thought it was hysterical.

"She doesn't want lessons," he told everyone. "She says she's done it and doesn't have to do it again! Isn't that a riot?" It was a wonderful giddy time.

I remember a trip we took to Hawaii with his three teenage daughters from another marriage. One day he took me in a golf cart high up onto the side of a mountain that seemed to over-look the entire world. We were literally above the clouds and I felt that way with him at that moment, although I will also say that when it started to rain, I insisted we stop puttering around in that golf cart and he take me back to the hotel. Even in the rain, it was difficult to get him to leave the golf course.

But I had my ways on that Hawaii trip. One day, I steered Vic away from the course by herding him and his daughters down to a boat I had rented for the afternoon. He looked wor-ried. "How long are we going to be out at sea?" he asked.

"Not too long," I promised. But we stayed out for most of the day. The sea was so gorgeous that day, beautiful swells against the rocky, tropical coastline, and occasionally flying fish leaping in front of the bow. I love to fish. I love being out at sea, far from any telephone or fax machine, and looking out at the clouds and the horizon. Something is always happening in the water. It rises and falls and surges, and if you pay attention you can see dolphins or whales, or follow the patterns of sea-birds. I was in a big hat and bigger sunglasses, deep in conversa-tion with one of Vic's daughters, when my line went taut, and the next thing I knew, everyone was around me yelling and helping me pull something in. I put my weight into it (and I was much thinner then) and yanked up a big silver monster of a fish, a tuna, shiny as a quarter. We laughed all the way to shore.

That evening, we were all getting dressed to have dinner in the hotel restaurant, where our fish would be prepared for us. And it was just the most wonderful moment. There's nothing like the feeling you get when you wash the sea off of your body after a day in the salt air, and dress up for dinner. We were all so happy that evening. Although I think Vic would have been happier if he didn't learn that the hotel was charging us two hundred and fifty dollars to prepare the fish I caught.

"That's ridiculous," he said.

"What are you going to do, Damone?" is all I said.

This was around 1986, my happy *Dynasty* period, when all my worries about my career were at bay and I was submerged in the pageantry of big hair and bigger shoulders. Joan Collins and I had been friends for a long time. In fact, just a couple of years earlier, in 1983, we were at a party at my New York apartment, wondering what the hell to do with our careers. Now all worries were gone. We were in a show so successful and fluffy that nobody on the set could have any serious problems. I'll never forget the day a director said to Catherine Oxenberg, "You know, this is not open-heart surgery. Just say your lines so that we can all go home." The only problems we ever had were if Joan thought her costume looked too much like mine or Linda's. Then there'd be a gale-force wind of clothing changes that left the dressing-room floor looking as if a hurricane had come through and taken down a dress shop. Hair and makeup? Bring it on, please!

I loved my role of Dominique Deveraux, television's first black bitch. My character was introduced to the series at the end of the third season. I had asked Aaron Spelling to write me into the show. He thought it was a great idea. But it didn't happen overnight. In fact, months went by and I heard nothing about my idea moving forward. I think I actually sealed it on the night of the Golden Globes. I had just sung a love song from *Yentl* at the awards dinner at the request of none other than Barbra Streisand, who, I guess, knew that I am often told I have a half-Jewish soul! *Dynasty* got plenty of awards that night after its second season, and I was in such a great mood after singing to such a powerful room of show-business honchos that I threw caution to the wind along with everything I knew about etiquette. I had heard Aaron Spelling was having a private party with his *Dynasty* cast and crew to celebrate. So I went to the restaurant, uninvited. Happily, Aaron told me he was delighted to see me and had been seriously thinking about a part for me on *Dynasty.* After that, the doors flew open and I was in. Sometimes you have to break rules to get what you need. Although I do feel that it's also important that you know the rules before you break them.

When we started discussing my *Dynasty* part with Aaron's writers, I told them I wanted them to write a character for me as if they were writing for a rich white man. They did, and I had a ball! It was fine with me that race didn't figure into my character. I came out of an era with Bobby Short and Lena Horne, a time in which black performers strove for a kind of acceptability that a large part of the black community still encouraged in their role models. In the late sixties, when I played Julia, a single working mother who was very smooth around the edges, I was suddenly accused of being a "white folks' nigger" by people who weren't comfortable with the show. (People either loved or hated it.) I always despised that. But I never saw myself as compromising. I sang the music I loved and accepted the roles that appealed to me. And what a relief it was to be able to play a believable black bitch divested of any politics at all.

Dynasty was shot in the era of old-school network television, with gargantuan staffs and budgets. It was always such a pleasure driving onto the ABC lot to go to work in the morning only to be babied and pampered for hours. Vic could do what he liked best all day—play golf. And I could do what I liked best, work. We had a lot of laughs. One day, we three leading ladies were asked to do an awards show together, and the wardrobe designer wanted all of us in white. Joan was not having any of it. So while she went backstage to commandeer a different outfit, I talked Linda Evans into playing a little trick when she returned. While rehearsing at the podium, we kept shifting places to prevent Joan from placing herself in between us. We completely upset her natural tendency to always be center stage. Joan has a great sense of humor. And we had such a sense of victory during the run of that show. All three of us were deep into middle age, yet ruling the ratings as television stars.

I wonder if that caused problems for my relationship with Vic. Well, I was on a hit television show, and I was performing "one-nighters" (singing engagements) whenever the opportunity arose. I was an incredibly hard worker. Vic was none of the above. Early on, long before we were married, he was having dinner with me when he started talking about the problems he was having paying for his house in Palm Springs. I thought that was kind of strange, but no major alarm bells went off in my head. Bells didn't go off in London, either, when he decided that despite the fact that we had tickets to the theater, he really wasn't interested in going, just as he refused to go to see Pavarotti with me one night in Los Angeles because he couldn't miss a baseball game on television. I like sports on television, but I wasn't sure I wanted to be married to a sports addict. By the time the alarm bells finally sounded loud and clear, it was too late.

A couple years into our relationship, after I helped him pay off his Palm Springs home, Vic proposed to me in the bedroom of my house in Beverly Hills. By then, he'd already moved in. I was completely under his spell. And of course it was so lovely to have a companion to sleep with and plan things with and go out with. I don't remember the exact words, but our conversation was surprisingly profound. We were both talking about how taken aback we were at the depth of our feelings for each other. I mean we weren't children. We'd both been around the block, with a half dozen marriages between us. But we really did love each other, so we decided to get married.

I suppose that's when the real trouble started. A few days before the wedding, we were performing at a hotel in the Catskills. We were doing a show together by then, sharing a bill, but keeping our egos in check by switching whose name would go first on advertising for each venue. I was surprised that he cared. As usual, he was far more concerned about playing golf than rehearsing. "I have a tee-off at noon," he'd say.

"But we have an orchestra to rehearse," I'd reply.

"You go ahead, you know the act." And off he went with his golf buddies.

It made me more than anxious. It infuriated me. I'd always surrounded myself with consummate professionals, who took pleasure in the hard work of getting things exactly right. Vic was something else entirely. He relied on his charm and his lovely voice, and expected to be given a pass on any real work. He left it to me to hold things together, and make sure all the pieces fell into place for every show. And I never spoke to him about this irresponsible behavior. Something about him didn't allow me to think clearly as an adult. He always created a kind of whirlwind around us that threw me off balance. But our show always came off well. We'd sing romantic songs to each other, and saunter across the stage arm in arm, like a couple of kids in love. The truth is that as tense as he could make me, we were still terribly giddy together, and I loved watching him do his thing onstage and he loved watching me do mine. The audiences adored us this way, looking gaga for each other. Our big number was "How Do You Keep the Music Playing?" Later, when we were so angry that we could hardly stand on the same stage together, it would become a very good question.

Our wedding was to be in Atlantic City, where we were performing. As much as I'm a control freak, and completely capable of running my life, selling houses, taking care of finances, I never have control of myself around men. I knew our relationship wasn't ideal. But I didn't stop to think about what an impending fourth marriage really meant. That's not to say I didn't almost call the whole thing off when Vic decided not to travel with me from our Catskills job to Atlantic City because he wanted to spend another day on the golf course.

"We have a show and a wedding in three days," I pleaded. "What is this about?"

"My friends are telling me you have too much control over me," he said.

"What are you talking about? You can do whatever you want, Vic."

"What will our marriage be like if I can't play golf when I like?"

"But we have so much to do in the next three days. Please!"

"No, Diahann. My friends are laughing at me, and I'm going to stay to play golf."

I was so furious that when I got to our suite in Atlantic City, I had the management padlock the door, and I remember thinking, "Oh my God, this is so embarrassing." Then, when he finally arrived, our friends and family got us together for a crisis intervention. I remember everyone sitting together in my suite and politely asking if we really wanted to go through with the wedding. If we were discussing anything else, real estate, a show, a management question, I would have been levelheaded and seen things clearly and called it off. I mean, I was fifty years old by then. But I still had no idea how to express my true feelings when it came to men. Surely I knew that it would have been better to have an affair with this man than to marry him?

"Diahann," my good friend Amy had told me, "he doesn't read books! What are you doing?"

What *was* I doing? Competing with Elizabeth Taylor in husband collecting?

At any rate, it was too late to stop it, or so I thought at the time. The press was coming to Atlantic City to cover the wedding, print and television. All our guests were arriving. Somehow we kissed and made up and went on with the show. That wedding really was a show, all about our outfits and hair and makeup. It was mostly his friends, and just a few of mine with my family. And officiating was a minister who looked like he was straight out of Central Casting. "Who is this man marrying us?" I kept thinking. "Where did he come from?" Then we went and played lovers onstage in the casino. There's one line in "How Do You Keep the Music Playing?" that asks the most important question. "How do you lose yourself to someone and never lose your way?" I wish I could have figured that one out then and there.

The truth is, as I've said, I have never been levelheaded around men.

In fact, I look back on my behavior now and wonder what the hell I was thinking. Maybe that's what happens when you become a senior citizen. You see yourself with clarity for

the first time in your life. After so many unsuccessful relationships that put me at my worst, I'm glad to finally be on my
own.

I mean, for God's sake, I was dating a married man when I
was nineteen! James Edwards was a beautiful man and a very
good actor. He was also an alcoholic. I would wait in my hotel
room in Los Angeles, after long days of shooting *Carmen Jones*,
hoping he would call. If and when the phone finally rang, he'd
demand that I meet him downstairs in twenty minutes. He was
always angry at the powers that be—roles for him did not come
as he wanted them to. He made it his business to brag about
dalliances with wives of producers he was meeting for lunch the
next day. Why was I so bedazzled? To my still-maturing mind,
he seemed so in control, so confident. At the time, I was still so
skinny and devoid of sexuality that I didn't think of myself as
attractive. Suddenly here was this handsome movie star court-
ing me. How could I keep a level head?

One Saturday night, he led me upstairs to a bedroom at
the hotel in which he was staying and told me to take off my
clothes. I stripped to my undergarments, totally confused, as he
stared at me from a chair across the room. Then he got up to
leave me alone. "You stay here," he said. "I'll let you know when
you can go." He closed the door and I heard him locking it from
outside with a key. I remained there for hours, waiting passively.
He didn't come for me until the next day. But I never screamed,
"How dare you!" or that we were finished. This was definitely a
lack-of-self-esteem issue.

Broadway rescued me from him. When *Carmen Jones* was
over, I left James Edwards and Los Angeles behind, and took

the red-eye back to New York for my second audition for the ingenue role in *House of Flowers*. On my way from the airport, I stopped to get my hair styled and dozed off in the chair. When I awoke, I looked in the mirror and screamed. I looked like a little boy. I apologized when I got to the theater. But out from the darkness I heard Truman Capote's eerily high Southern drawl. "Oh, don't apologize," he said. "Your hair is just marvelous, it couldn't be more perfect." Then I sat down at the edge of the stage and charmed my way into the part. Maybe it was the jet lag. But it could have been that my time in Hollywood had relaxed me just enough.

The casting director was a handsome man named Monte Kay. He had rejected me the first time I auditioned. But when we were performing the show in Philadelphia, he came backstage to praise my performance and he asked me out to dinner. Looking very cosmopolitan in a well-cut gray suit, he carried himself with confident ease. I had my first taste of oysters and clams on the half shell with him that night. I loved his face, rugged, with a strong nose and a dimple on the chin. Clearly, there was a mutual attraction, although I was as innocent as he was worldly. Well, he was eleven years my senior. He was also white. But how was I to know? He was dark with extremely curly hair, after all. When a friend told me otherwise, I was shocked. I ran to the phone.

"Monte, are you white?" I asked him.

"Yes, and I'm Jewish, too," he answered. "Is that all right?"

I couldn't think of a reason why it wasn't, unless of course I thought about what my parents might think. He was divine.

He made me laugh, and feel like a grown-up after my disastrous and strange relationship in Hollywood with an alcoholic married man.

"But why are you so brown?" I asked.

"Because I love the sun and I love my sunlamp," he said. "I like being tan."

He had also loved being around musicians ever since he was a kid and would sneak into Greenwich Village from Brooklyn to hear jazz. He went to churches to hear gospel music, too. While still in his teens, he produced concerts featuring Charlie Parker and Dizzy Gillespie. Then he went on to open the nightclub Birdland, and to manage the brilliant Modern Jazz Quartet. For him, my race was no problem; in fact, just the opposite. When my mother saw how wonderful he was to me, and how caring and amused he was by me (even though I was a clueless child compared with everyone else he knew), she knew she had to take us seriously. So she arranged for Monte and me to meet with Adam Clayton Powell, by then a congressman, to have a serious conversation about our situation. It turned out that Monte and Adam were old pals from Birdland. Adam offered to perform the wedding ceremony for us in his home. We accepted. But my father did not find the interracial marriage acceptable. He had little trust for the white community, and felt I had betrayed him terribly. It broke my heart when he didn't attend the wedding in 1956.

Eventually, Dad came around, when he saw what a good man Monte was, thoughtful and very supportive of my career. But I started having my own problems with my marriage right

away. We were in Los Angeles after our wedding, and one morning I woke up in our room at the Beverly Hilton. Monte was outside on the balcony reading a book. He ignored me when I called
out to him. I knew he could lose himself in his reading, but for
some reason, on that day it unnerved me. I mean, this was the
first time I had ever been away with a man—this was our
honeymoon—and my husband, who I was to remain with for
the rest of my life—was ignoring me. I felt a chasm open up in
front of me, between us, like the fault line where an earthquake
occurs. I have to say, it's all so laughable now. I had a smart husband, a kind man who loved to read. What was wrong with that?
I've known so many swaggering men since Monte who didn't
read, and were so anti-intellectual that it made me yearn for
someone with a brain. But what did I know at twenty-one years
old? I stormed out to the balcony to pull Monte off his book, and
engage him. He kept reading. I pressed up against him, and all
he did was glare at me and go back to his pages.

I guess I was supposed to remain quiet until he was ready
to talk. Instead, I ran back into the room, dove onto the bed,
and banged my fist against the walls.

"Why don't you like me?" I screamed. "Why won't you
speak to me?"

Monte was shocked. He'd always been able to retreat into
his reading, and the women he'd been with before accepted his
need for quiet. Not me. I wanted attention when I wanted it. I
pounded the walls and carried on until he looked up.

"What's the matter with you, Diahann? What do you want
from me?" he asked.

"Anything! I'll take anything," I said. "Just answer me when I talk to you!"

"I'll answer you later. You can see I'm reading."

"You can't ignore me like this!"

I'm still not sure what caused this outburst from me. I was a young bride and I wanted to assert myself, I suppose, and although I'd been raised to be polite, I'd also been raised to feel that I was a special little princess. Maybe my dreadful affair with James Edwards just a couple years before had made me overly sensitive. Oh, who knows what was wrong with me? At the time, I thought nothing, that this was all Monte's fault.

Fifty years and four marriages later, I know the fault was mine.

We did love each other, even as we disagreed, and we did want to make it work. So I tried to be less demanding and he tried to be more attentive. We bought an apartment on Tenth Avenue in Manhattan, and I threw myself into decorating it as if it were the only thing in the world that mattered to me. Monte was surprised and so were his friends. They wondered aloud, "Who's this bourgeois girl he married, obsessed with the furniture department at Macy's and chattering on about appliances and window treatments?" When the apartment was totally decorated, I went back out on singing jobs.

Three years after I got married, I was singing at a club called the Black Orchid in Chicago (where I almost walked off the stage because a man in the audience was heckling me with racist remarks) when an offer came for me to play a supporting role in the film version of *Porgy and Bess*. I didn't want to do it. I liked being the star of my own show, and didn't see the point of being in the background, especially of another film with more predictable scenes of a tawdry impoverished life on Catfish Row. But Monte insisted it would be good for my career. I suppose it was. But it wreaked havoc on my marriage and the next ten years of my life. It was on the set of that movie that I met Sidney Poitier.

FOUR

Men, Take Two

IT'S NICE TO FIND I HAVE A SENSE OF HUMOR ABOUT
"l'Affair Poitier" now, from the comfort of my golden years.
When I look back on it, I can only shake my head and perhaps even make the *tsk, tsk* sound the elders used to make
during my South Carolina summers. What the hell was I
thinking? Actually, I wasn't. I was letting someone else think
for me, a habit that was really becoming my specialty act
around men.

It was 1959. I was sitting at the office of Samuel Goldwyn
to receive the new production schedule for *Porgy and Bess,* when
he walked in—this incredibly beautiful jet-black man with the
fierce eyes and the smooth gait of a panther. Cheekbones beyond fabulous. I immediately became anxious and kept crossing and uncrossing my legs as if I were doing some kind of
cancan. I was sure he could see, and maybe even smell my discomfort. He exuded such sexuality and such commanding
power that I felt completely unmoored in his presence. He went

around the room shaking hands, telling people, "I'm Sidney Poitier," as if they didn't know the biggest black sensation in the world. He was a confident, brilliant man who, despite many accomplishments, had so many more to come, including being appointed ambassador to Japan from the Bahamas. Unlike James Edwards and others before him, he would not and could not be stopped by his race.

"I've looked forward to working with you," he told me. Then he held me at length with both his arms, as if to suggest I was his captive. "We must talk."

"Yes," I squeaked.

I couldn't believe what I was feeling. I was a faithfully married woman. Sidney was married, too, and with children. But he was such a big star by then that all kinds of women had been throwing themselves at him. I, on the other hand, was anything but overtly sexual. Casual sex was out of the question for a white-glove-wearing girl like me. The cast of *Porgy and Bess* was staying at the Chateau Marmont in Hollywood, and it was like a dormitory, with all of us eating and socializing together. I tried to avoid him as much as possible and at the same time was giddy thinking I might run into him. I might have been an actress, but I was fooling nobody pretending he didn't rock my world. But I guess it was the restraint of the clean and well-mannered young lady so carefully trained by her mother that eventually got to him. One day, he walked into my dressing room, surprising me so that I jumped from my chair.

"Diahann," he said in a voice that was something between

a growl and a purr. "I'm having dinner with Ruby Dee and some friends tonight. Would you join us?"

"That sounds lovely," I said. I should have known he had something more intimate in mind when he suggested he pick me up rather than meet me at the restaurant.

We arrived together, a handsome couple trying too hard to be incognito. Everyone in the entire room turned and stared. Ruby, who, with her husband, Ossie Davis, was close to Sidney and his wife, did not look comfortable with what she was seeing. We escalated from there to more dates, my attraction growing stronger and stronger. I was smitten, fascinated, and scared. One night when he walked me up to my room, I locked myself in the bathroom and told him I was taking a bath and good night, just to prevent anything from happening. Another time I hid in the closet when he came in looking for me. Desperate to stop myself from disaster, I invited Monte out for the weekend. We had a terrible time. I was too mesmerized by Sidney to enjoy sharing a bed with my own husband. "I don't know what's wrong with you," Monte said at the end of three days. "But that was the worst weekend of my life."

Monte was unhappy, and to my surprise, Sidney was furiously jealous, even though he was married.

But he had other things on his mind. The movie was under fire for being stereotyped and insulting to blacks. This was the reason I had not wanted to be involved in the first place. He was very political and very articulate about his opinions. And just as he wouldn't be pushed around by any woman, he would not be pushed around by any press agent or studio boss. He certainly wouldn't allow any journalist to railroad him into conversations about the issues swirling around the *Porgy and Bess* set.

Not long ago, I was in Manhattan with a friend who begged me to go with him to a special screening of *Porgy and Bess* at the Ziegfeld Theater. A film historian had found a special print of it, and when we arrived, someone was giving a passionate speech.

"Movie musicals today are made by people who don't like musicals," this man was telling a small audience that was completely devoid of blacks. "You have to readjust your viewing strategies because this film has the pace of yesterday."

That's not all it had of yesterday. When the credits stopped rolling and the camera started panning across a dock of hardworking black folk on a bayou, I squirmed in my seat at the sight of this cliché of noble poverty as reimagined by some very talented white men, including Otto Preminger, the director, and, of course, George Gershwin. It should be said that, as Jews, they were sympathetic to the status of blacks as "others." The trouble was, their sympathy felt demeaning. And walking among all those hardworking plain folk carrying their baskets of shrimp and fish, and humming to something that almost sounded like a spiritual (but as reinvented by a wonderful Jewish composer) was a slim young girl in a ratty ankle-length dress, holding a little baby. The girl opened her mouth to sing, and out of it came the most beautiful and wistful song: "Summertime and the living is easy!"

Never mind that her voice was dubbed because the original key was written for a soprano. The lovely young woman was none other than me. But unfortunately, it was a little hard to tell because I was wearing a large bandanna on top of my head. It was as hideous a look as I ever had to endure, and all the more annoying after my recent glamorous appearances in nightclubs and on television. But it really didn't matter to me that I had to wear that bandanna. I had agreed to be in a picture that I didn't even want black children (who were struggling with the cruelties of segregation in the South at the time) to see. It was 1959 in America, when Miles Davis, a friend and neighbor of mine in Manhattan, was redefining the jazz idiom internationally, Lorraine Hansberry was writing landmark plays, and Nina Simone was singing "Young, Gifted and Black," and this movie was depicting us as poor, uneducated, drug-dealing, libidinous, and totally unsophisticated. This big-deal, big-budget movie was doing nothing to depict blacks in a positive light. Rather, it was throwing us back. But the music? It was divine!

So I did as I was told and wore the bandanna. "Your career is coming along nicely," I reminded myself daily, "and soon this film will be over and you can go back to your pearls and evening gowns." Then, one day on the set, Mr. Preminger said with his German accent, "Why are you always wearing that thing on your head? We can't see you." So I took the thing off for the rest of the shoot that day.

The next thing I knew I was being summoned to see Samuel Goldwyn, the producer. His wife, Frances, met me outside his office. She was adorable, a housewife who wanted to work, and she was flustered about something. It was hard to take her seriously. As I recall, my visit started with her admiring the elegant capri pants I was wearing, and I thought to myself, "This is going to be the dumbest conversation of my life." But then she stopped with the chitchat and got a very concerned look on her face, as if the situation were dire.

"You do know why you're here today, don't you, Diahann?" she said.

I told her I had no idea.

"Mr. Goldwyn went berserk when he saw the rushes."

"Why? What happened?"

"You weren't wearing your bandanna!"

"Oh, that's right, so what is the plan?"

"He wants to see you" is all she said.

So we went into the most ostentatious office I have ever seen. Mr. Goldwyn was a little man who was sitting in a chair as big as a throne. He hardly took a moment to greet me before he said, "I am not going to allow you to ruin this film!"

I knew better than to ask why until he had finished spouting.

"You cannot make decisions about your wardrobe or hair or anything else unless it goes through your director!"

In a calm voice, hiding my fear, I asked what exactly he was talking about.

"This is not the place for you to decide that you look better without a head scarf," he barked at me. "All you have to do is do as you're told!"

He may have been justifiably upset, but that was no way to talk to a Harlem princess. I was now trembling, and I knew I had to be careful because I had a reputation of being kind of fresh, not difficult, just strong-willed. So I looked him in the eye and said, "I'm sorry, Mr. Goldwyn, but even my own father would never speak to me in that manner." I saw Frances Goldwyn's jaw drop. Sam Goldwyn's face remained stonelike. "But if you'd like to discuss the scarf, I'd be happy to tell you what happened."

Fortunately, I didn't have to, because at that moment Otto Preminger came in and told Mr. Goldwyn that removing the head scarf had been his idea, not mine.

"You really should let her go home now," he said.

He was protecting me, but he was also protecting his production. He knew I was a feisty little lady. "Don't worry about this at all," Otto said as he walked me to my car.

"You know I would never do anything you don't tell me to do," I told him.

"I'll take care of everything," he said.

If only he could have taken care of how ridiculous the whole movie was, with its silly squalor, Sammy Davis Jr. hopping around like a blue jay, dancing and selling cocaine, Pearl Bailey talking like a strident, trashy black woman, and most of all, Sidney on strange little knee crutches, making moon eyes at Dorothy Dandridge.

"Bess, you is my woman now," he pretended to sing in a basso profundo.

Well, I have to say, only Sidney was beautiful enough to pull off being a sex symbol who crawled around on the floor. He had those aforementioned cheekbones, and he just reeked of nobility and dignity, even amid all that art-directed Negro squalor.

What can I say? It didn't work for me then and it still doesn't now.

I sat through the recent *Porgy and Bess* screening in New York for a while. But it became too tedious. So I got up with my friend and we quietly ditched the Ziegfeld Theater.

In Los Angeles, it was a lot harder to ditch Sidney. Toward the end of the filming, after weeks of meeting for dinner, finding time for quiet walks, Sidney and I were taking a walk near the Chateau one night when he grabbed me.

"All right! All right! I love you," he said.

"And I love you, too," I replied.

We finally said it. And we kissed, then we held each other tight and cried.

"What are we going to do?" I asked.

He didn't know. He loved me, but he loved his wife, who was a good mother and, to make matters more difficult, a good Catholic. She had stuck with him through his worst years. Now, he said, she would ruin him and take his children, too. I said that I would not be able to have an affair while married to Monte, and would have to leave him first. After the movie wrapped, we would both be back in New York. Sidney was going to be in *A Raisin in the Sun*. I wanted to audition, too, but he was not encouraging me. He simply could not imagine that a woman would want a career in show business. "Diahann, what is the point?" he once said, sighing. Strange as it sounds for an actor, he hated anything that suggested artifice, even the promotional photos for my nightclub act.

"What is all this makeup?" he said. "You look ridiculous."

I was too flustered to do good work in front of him at my

audition for *A Raisin in the Sun,* and didn't get the part. But gossip was spreading. Monte worried that it was true. "Are you involved with Sidney Poitier?" he asked. The truth was I wasn't. It would be several years before we acted on our attraction.

Sidney did his Broadway play. I went back to singing, and was so grateful that Monte helped me negotiate my contracts to sing at the Plaza's Persian Room. Meanwhile, though we had traded Los Angeles for New York, Sidney and I continued to see each other. He would call me at home and hang up if Monte answered the phone. We'd meet at sleazy Times Square movie houses. After months of talk, we finally decided that Sidney would leave his wife and I would leave my husband and check into the Waldorf-Astoria. He would register at another hotel. The morning I was leaving our apartment on Tenth Avenue, Monte was next to me in bed. I abruptly turned to him and said, "I've fallen in love with Sidney Poitier, and I'm leaving you." He kicked me to the floor. Then he began to cry. We both did. I packed my things with my head spinning, feeling nauseous and so weak that it was difficult to lift even the lightest item.

When Sidney arrived at the hotel that night, he did something very strange. He looked over at my small suitcase and asked, "Is that all you brought? You don't plan to stay very long, do you?" He was suddenly in a frenzy. "I knew you wouldn't be able to really leave your marriage," he barked. "I knew you wouldn't do it!" It was very confusing, until I asked him the name of his hotel and realized he had not moved out of his house in Westchester. Nor did he tell his wife he wanted a divorce. I was too upset to say anything, and too paralyzed to take any action. I heard traffic below us on Park Avenue, and yearned to be out there on the street rather than trapped in this situation. But I just sat there, all nerves, but in silence. Finally Sidney looked at his watch and said he needed to be home to help put his children to bed. At three in the morning, I called Monte. He wasn't asleep. He said to come home to talk.

I did, and discovered that while Monte was hurt, it helped for him to know I had never slept with Sidney. Maybe we could reconcile. Later, Sidney called.

"Of course you went home, didn't you," he said. "You never intended to leave your husband." He couldn't possibly be serious.

"How can you say that?" I told him. "I did what I was supposed to do."

We agreed to get on with things, this time for real. So I went back to the Waldorf for a few days, but Sidney did not come. Again, I went home to Monte, humiliated and devastated. My mother was shocked when I told her my marriage was in trouble. But both she and Monte's sister felt that a baby would be the answer to this problem, that it would bring me down to earth and stabilize the marriage.

And that's what happened. Monte was wonderful during the pregnancy. So was everyone else, including Marilyn Monroe. When I was performing at a posh club in Los Angeles called Mocambo, I sat down with her and a movie executive named Max Youngstein after a show. Marilyn, who wanted a baby so badly, looked at me and put her hand on my belly. "You must be so happy," she said with a sigh. I was, and Monte was ecstatic the day I put his hand on my stomach and he felt the baby kick for the first time. But I also knew we weren't out of trouble. I hadn't spoken to Sidney for months. But one day when I was close to giving birth, I bumped into him on Fifty-seventh Street.

"You were never supposed to have anyone's child but mine," he said.

He walked away before I could even say, "Good line, Sidney!"

The birth of my daughter, in 1961, was not easy, but when she was finally out, I was ecstatic to be a mother. We were all ecstatic. But I also knew deep down that nothing had changed for me and my feelings about my marriage. I was standing in the hospital when I told my mother, "I'm going to leave Monte."

"Oh no, I thought that was over," she said.

"I love my baby and I care about Monte, but I can't stay with him," I said.

"Are you leaving because of Sidney?" she asked.

"I don't know," I said. "But I have to move on."

We didn't separate immediately. For a while, things stayed the same. I went back to singing. My engagement at the Plaza continued to make me happy, as did fussing over my infant. The only problem I ever had at the Plaza was the time that management told me they didn't think I should be singing a song by Oscar Brown Jr. called "Brown Baby." Two executives reported to me that some people in the audience found the lyrics offensive.

Brown baby, as you grow up,
I want you to drink from the plenty cup . . .

It was a lovely lullaby to sing to a child about living with a
head held high in a better world. I told the executives that I sang
this song for my baby daughter. "This is not an offensive lyric,
it's a dream for my child," I said. I was careful not to embarrass
them. But I said, "We can't let audiences dictate what I'm going
to sing." And I prevailed. It was another instance of my ability
to keep control of any situation involving anything other than
love and men. I took my singing very seriously, and would not
have it compromised. Singing always got me through my life,
and it always would.

Suzanne was four months old when I received a screenplay. It was for *Paris Blues,* a kind of double romance about two
expatriate musicians and a couple of vacationing teachers from
the United States. I wanted to do it. It had a social awareness
that was very compelling and it showed two sophisticated black
characters that would be just the thing to move the national
conversation along. I got the part, and ended up playing Joanne
Woodward's sidekick. Guess who played Paul Newman's? Sidney. I thought it would be fine. I'd grown up and had a baby,
and Sidney had a new one, too.

Monte didn't want me to do the film and be in Paris with
Sidney, but he also knew that roles like this didn't come along
often. The baby, at four months, was too young to travel. I left
her with him and flew to France, my mind reeling all the while.
When I got there, I calmed down. It was so wonderful to watch
Joanne Woodward at work. Seeing the rushes of one of her

scenes, I heard Marty Ritt, the director, remark about the wonderful things she could do in front of a camera. He was right. I watched how she could just stand still and conjure exactly what it took to make a scene work. I was studying diligently at the Actors Studio in those years (and Marlon Brando had sent me boxes of books on the craft of acting) and I had developed as an actress. Watching Joanne deepened my conviction, and I carried some of my new confidence to my scenes with Sidney. I think he sensed I was growing as an artist and growing up as a woman.

But I was not grown up enough to know how to control myself. And neither was he. One night we decided to get it out of the way and go ahead and finally sleep together. I was petrified and it was a total disaster. "What is the matter with you?" he asked.

"I don't know. But being with you like this makes me feel like trash," I replied.

"You want too much," he told me.

Perhaps. But after that I did my best to not wait around for my phone to ring. One night, Duke Ellington, who was working on the music for the film, took me out and fed me caviar. He treated me beautifully, and it's exactly what I needed at that moment. He must have seen that I was missing something in my life. Maybe it would change when Monte and my parents came over from New York with the baby at the end of filming. I was desperate to have little Suzanne with me. When she arrived in my mother's arms at Orly Airport, I could barely control my hysteria. I was still so young. Young enough, actually, to have originally named my child Ottille, based on the character I played in *House of Flowers*. Does that give you some insight into my immature, narcissistic little mind? I may have done things wrong raising my daughter, but at least I knew enough to change her name to something far more reasonable a few years later. Ottille. Oy! What was I thinking? At any rate, I was thrilled to finish the movie with her nearby. It was her first road trip with me. My family was so happy to be in Paris. But even as my mother ran around in a giddy state, preparing for festive holidays, Monte and I remained estranged. Meanwhile, Sidney and I met in secret and took long walks in the cold damp Paris nights, not unlike the ones we took in the movie along the Seine, very glum and noir. We decided that something really had to be done and came up with a plan.

After Paris, we would send our families home and then call them from Sweden (who knows why—maybe because it's such a progressive country) with our news. Guess what? It never happened. Sidney got called in at the last minute to be part of the Kennedy inauguration gala. He'd have to rush home right away. So there was to be no divorce announcement, and no further plans. I ended up flying home alone.

Months later, he met with Monte and me after one of my shows in New York.

"I'm in love with your wife," Sidney told him. "It's been going on for years. Perhaps we should bring this to a head now so we can all rebuild our lives. I've talked to my wife and we're getting a divorce. I think it would be better for everyone if you and Diahann did the same." Monte looked stricken, but said, "Well, if that's what Diahann wants, I won't stand in her way."

So we finally went and got our divorce. It was amicable. I wanted him to be a part of Suzanne's life and I was still fond of him.

Monte moved out of the apartment and Sidney and I started dating for real, and it was wonderful. One night when he called, I knew it would finally be the night we'd make love. I finally chose a black sheath to wear with no jewelry at all—the look of simple elegance I was finding for myself in those years. I had my hair done and I took a long bath, and came out looking adorable and immaculate. Sidney appeared, looking wonderful, and that night we made love, finally, and it was passionate and perfect. Our relationship suddenly blossomed, and we had some wonderful weeks together. But eventually, it became clear that he had done nothing about his divorce. Was I that foolish that I still had hopes he would? Could I really have been that frightened of being alone for even a month?

I asked him why he was not divorcing, as he'd promised so often.

"Diahann, you just don't understand. You're such an ingrate," he said.

"Sidney, we're back at the same old place again," I said.

"Because you keep putting us there," he said.

I continued to see Sidney. He seduced the entire cast of *No Strings* with his charm when he came to see us in tryouts. And I almost got fired from the show when I got a call from him from a movie set in Yugoslavia and he told me he needed me to come right away. Richard Rodgers was furious, but I went, a long exhausting flight, only to find Sidney cold and uncommunicative when I finally arrived. One night, the cast of his movie was singing at a piano bar. I asked if I could join them. "Diahann," he said, "every black person can either dance or sing, and I wish you'd stop." He still had no respect for me, and he sent me home from Europe tourist class. I should have clobbered him for the way he was treating me. But each time he hurt me, I just bounced back as if nothing were the matter, as if I didn't mind being abused and hurt on a regular basis.

Maybe my trouble was that my parents had always deferred to people they perceived as more powerful than themselves. Or was it that all those years ago my parents left me in South Carolina, and I'd had abandonment issues ever since? All I knew was I had chosen a man who was totally unavailable.

It's always the same. Around men, I don't like myself much.

Time passed. I dated my road manager, when *No Strings* went on a national tour. Sidney called my hotel in Los Angeles and woke up my mother and daughter.

"You bitch, whore, tramp," he yelled. "I know he just left your bed. I won't have you running around with other men. You belong to me!"

We fought until—lo and behold—on the spur of the moment he decided he'd buy me a ring and fly to Mexico for his divorce. Stupid as it sounds, I believed it, and told my mother. "Oh no," she said. "Where will this end?"

He bought me the ring. He got the divorce in Mexico. Then he flew to Utah to make a western with James Garner. I went back to New York to decorate a ten-room apartment on Riverside Drive that he had purchased. I was only home a few days when he called to say his wife was having second thoughts. Our wedding plans would have to be postponed. This time it didn't bother me so much. Therapy was helping me understand myself a little better, and the more liberal current of the times allowed me to appreciate the out-of-wedlock relationship we had. I thought we'd eventually marry. But when the apartment was ready and I was about to move my daughter in with me, Sidney told me he didn't want her there, even though she'd been part of the plans from the start.

He changed the locks so I couldn't get in. Then he made me write him a check to offset his purchase and decorating costs. I did not even object. I did as I was told, submissive and desperate.

How did it end? In Nassau, where we had a lovers' spat, and quite a public one at that. In a busy harbor, with a friendly crowd watching us, he refused to let some adoring locals help him start the engine on our dinghy. He became very angry.

That's when I saw the real Sidney, as if for the first time. I suddenly understood his insecurities. I had always seen him as all-powerful. Suddenly I could see his flaws, and mine as well. And just like that, I knew it was over for real. Both of us knew, after nine years. Done! *Basta!* We said good-bye and we parted.

Did I learn anything from the whole decadelong dating debacle? Perhaps not, but I will say that Sidney and I are now friends. That's a lovely thing that comes as you age—forgiveness and perhaps a relaxing of standards just enough to give yourself and others a break. I'll never forget the time I ran into him after years of not seeing him. It was about ten years ago, and I had moved into my new condo, and I had a toothache that had me rushing off to the dentist. I was sitting in my Rolls waiting for someone to move the car blocking my way. I'm sure I was not looking my senior-glamorous best, without any makeup. I was in pain, after all, and my cheek was swollen and I was in a hurry to get going. So although I cringe now at the thought of being so impatient, I honked my horn. And out of the lobby doors came none other than Sidney. He looked over at me, nodded regally, and I couldn't hide. I was holding my hand to my cheek, in pain.

"I can't believe it! Sidney," I slurred. "You live here?"

He looked through my window, with a demonic grin. "Excuse me, ma'am," he joked at me. "Let me move my little car out of your way."

We both shook our heads and laughed, and whatever was left of my animosity fell away for good. Why hold each other responsible for what we did as children?

Not long ago, we were presenting together at an awards ceremony in New York. As we watched the young people scrambling all around us, people living at the white-hot center of things with long futures still ahead of them, we smiled like two contented grandparents. Sidney put his arm around me.

"Did I ever tell you how much I admire your work?" he said.

"No, I don't believe you ever did, Sidney," I replied. "But thank you."

There was another time when we ran into each other in my lobby. I was heading outside to my daughter's car. I guess Sidney had seen that she was out there waiting.

"Take my arm, Diahann," he commanded.

"What are you talking about? Why?" I asked.

"Just put your arm in mine and let's walk up to Suzanne and surprise her."

So I did as I was told. And my poor daughter saw me on the arm of this man who had been a large part of the problems of her childhood. We were standing right in front of her car.

She took one look at us and muttered, "Not *you* two again!"

We all had a laugh over that, a nice long one.

It's a shame I didn't have that kind of perspective on the relationships I found myself in after Sidney. A good laugh at the absurdity might have made things easier.

The years went by, male companions came and went. Alan Marshall was a handsome black actor, but no star. I'm sure the trappings of my life in my *Julia* years were part of my appeal to him. He moved into the mansion I had just bought while I was working on a singing tour between seasons of *Julia*. And he did so without my knowing it. This house in Beverly Hills had been owned by the son of Barbara Hutton, the famous Woolworth heiress. It was enormous, with its waterfall and swimming pool with a black bottom, unusual in those days. There was a large staff, a man in charge of cars, another in charge of the gardens, a nanny for my daughter, and a cook who didn't know how to cook. (I could only bring myself to fire her when she served game hens with the giblets still wrapped in paper in lieu of stuffing.) I once overheard Alan tell someone it was the home that I had bought for him. I let it go, as I chose to ignore all the signs that he was troubled, because, well, every princess needs her prince, and when I looked at us in the mirror, I thought I'd found mine. Okay, he was a little jealous.

But jealousy is one thing, verbal abuse is another. Instead of putting a stop to the verbal abuse for good, I let it continue. Then I started putting up with the physical abuse he doled out on a regular basis. The prospect of being alone was too unbearable for me at the time—until Sidney and I parted, I had never lived without a partner in all of my adult life, and here I was in my thirties! So I didn't show him that I had the slightest amount of self-respect. (Analysis eventually helped me recognize that living alone was something I needed to try. I now realize I didn't accomplish this until the end of my fourth marriage. Some of us are slow learners.) When I was with Alan, it was such a guilt-ridden time (*capitalist pigs* had entered the vernacular) that I thought it was possible I deserved to be treated badly just for being so wealthy. I was a big to-do at a cultural moment when monetary success was suspect. And when you're a success, it only makes the critics more shrill.

The question that kept coming up at the time was, "What kind of single black mother was I supposed to be as Julia anyway?" Twentieth Century-Fox and NBC expected the kind that got top Nielsen ratings! And yet the pressure to be someone else never let up in my three years on the show. I was not ignorant about the issues of civil rights in this country, or my place as a national celebrity who could voice opinions to help make changes. That's why I hosted fund-raisers for the Student Nonviolence Coordinating Committee with Harry Belafonte and Stokely Carmichael in my home. I supported the Black Panthers and Shirley Chisholm's bid to be the first black female president. In fact, her major Los Angeles fund-raiser was in my home. But deep down, I never saw *Julia* as a documentary, and I didn't see why, to be worthwhile, it had to be about a black woman wearing an Afro and dashiki and living in a ghetto. It was a sitcom. And it was a successful one. I knew why it was pulling in the ratings, too. It made the white majority feel comfortable with a black lead character who was not offensive to them in any way. And frankly, it was a role I was glad to portray.

Race, of course, is a major factor in my life, though it's never been my sole preoccupation. I grew up in schools with integrated classrooms. My mother constantly reminded me that I was not to be pushed into letting the color of my skin determine my entire life. I was trained by people who related to me based on my talent and ambition, not my race. I wasn't a sell-out, as I had been accused of being by some, but rather someone looking to do what I perceived as quality work.

Still, people wanted to know what kind of black woman I was. Oh, that question! Well, let's see: I was the kind of black woman who, when asked to play drums with Harry Belafonte on one of his specials, could not. After a few days of rehearsing a calypso song with him, well-meaning Harry discovered that I just could not beat a drum hanging around my neck and sing at the same time. And as much as he adored me, Harry had to accept that. What kind of black woman was I? The kind who went in front of advertisers and buyers at the "upfronts" before the first season of *Julia* and told them: "Hello, I'm Diahann Carroll, and I was raised by a nice Jewish family in Beverly Hills!" That broke the ice and got a laugh from the crowd. There were just so many questions to answer from the press in those years, and even as I took them on, I was apprehensive.

I was under the political microscope for *Julia* like you wouldn't believe. But I didn't have the expertise to discuss the socioeconomic situation of the African-American community. Nor did I feel I should have to defend the character of a polite nurse with excellent taste in clothes, some of which I brought to the set from my own closet. I was simply trying to get comfortable playing a hardworking, financially strapped single mother who slept on a living-room sofa in a one-bedroom apartment.

The studio had its hands full with all the complaint letters, and had to hire two full-time assistants just to answer all of them. And many psychologists, politicians, and journalists all felt it was important to meet with me about the show's impact.

I also had my hands full with Hal Kanter, the show's creator. He and I constantly discussed the material he was crafting. I was already established when *Julia* took me into the homes of millions. And when I inhabited a character, I did so completely—which, on occasion, brought me into conflict with Hal. He once wrote a scene in which I got so upset I tossed a baby into the air. As I confess in a later chapter, I'll never be given an award for mothering, but tossing a baby into the air is something I know a mother is not inclined to do. I told Hal so. He didn't want to change the script, and so he left the Fox lot. When I found out he was gone, I left the lot, too.

He called me in a rage. "What the hell are you doing?" he asked.

"What are you doing, Hal? Why did you leave the set?" A little give and a little take on both our parts and the scene worked out.

We had our issues, and despite the turmoil around America's first black sitcom, the show held up nicely. He really did write well. In the pilot episode, there's a scene in which Julia is on the phone with crotchety Dr. Chegley, the white doctor who's about to hire her, played by Lloyd Nolan.

"You should know I'm colored," she tells him.

"Oh, and what color are you?" he asks.

"I'm a Negro," Julia says.

"Have you always been a Negro or are you just trying to be fashionable?" he asks.

It was a great line, and an important one to air on national television at the time. But for every bit of good many felt the show was accomplishing, some felt the opposite.

Everything I said was making national news. Journalists tried to goad me into dismissing black nationalist groups and I absolutely refused. "Their purpose is to give dignity, education, and economic opportunity to young blacks, and that I support," I said.

Race was a part of Julia's life, but it didn't rule the show. Motherhood did. But people kept insisting that Julia was living a lie, and only dating the nicest black men. What did people expect? It was *network* television! Please!

One letter writer asked, "Don't you realize you're letting the white community get away with murder by not insisting it address itself to the black male?"

Actually, I had enough on my hands with the black male I had in my own life at the time. Flawed as he was in so many ways, Alan kept leading the chorus of critics. He knew what buttons to push. And I allowed it, defending myself against his accusations as if they were rational. His violence against me continued. I finally came to my senses the day he yelled at me in front of Suzanne.

It was especially ironic because it was in my house that he did so.

I took Suzanne and walked out on him then and there. When I returned the next day, he knocked me to the floor and kicked me in the face, shouting, "I will ruin your face!"

It was the worst beating he ever gave me, and it was the last. We were through.

And now for something completely different—David Frost, the television talk-show host who ruled the culture in the 1960s and 1970s. He was one of the best things that ever happened to me. We met in 1970, not long after the end of Alan, and while *Julia* was going into its third season. I was on hiatus, and singing in New York. He came backstage after my show, this suave, fair-skinned Englishman in a blue blazer and tie, and we ended up shooting pool with some friends. It was a lighthearted evening. Not long after that, he invited me to appear on his talk show. The hour flew. We had such a good time on the air that it felt like a first date. David put me totally at ease. We ended up being photographed out and about together in the weeks that followed, and it wasn't long before we realized we were getting quite serious.

The nights that followed were giddy, fizzy, and glossy. They were also very busy, as I was shooting *Julia* and David was hosting his talk shows in New York and London. But he always found a way to find me. "Darling, I have to fly into Los Angeles, tomorrow night—and we can have dinner, isn't that marvelous?" he'd say. And he'd be there, looking wonderful as we shared champagne. We were comfortable with each other. His family in England, whom he eventually took me to meet, was lovely and felt similar to mine—decent middle-class people with whom I could relate. In fact, I remember thinking his mother and mine were like black and white images of each other as they went off in their mink stoles together to the theater in New York. Like my mother, his mother had somehow created a famous son with a drive to charm millions.

And charm he did. My mother was crazy about him. Although she still didn't quite understand my ability to date men without concern for race.

"Don't you get confused when you wake up in the morning not knowing if the man next to you is going to be black or white?" she once asked me. "Mother, I don't go to bed with a color, I go to bed with a man!" I told her.

He was so kind to me and solicitous of her that her questions melted away.

It seemed there was nobody who didn't adore David and want him around, including the Nixons when they were in the White House. (Let it be known that I refused to go!) But I went just about everywhere else with him, and it could be exhausting, keeping up with his jet-set lifestyle. As our romance went public, we received constant coverage. But unlike the days when *The Bell Telephone Hour* called my agent to announce they would not consider me because I was married to Monte Kay, a white man, neither David nor I suffered consequences for our interracial relationship. In fact, Westinghouse, the broadcasting company that syndicated his show, was enthusiastic about us.

David was terribly supportive of my career. He listened as I worried aloud about what to do after *Julia*. One night, after we saw a brutal beating scene in the film *Klute*, I told him about Alan and the beatings I had received from him. He listened carefully, and caressed me. "Darling," he said, taking me in his arms as I cried, "there are certain things we must put behind us. That part of your life is over now, and you have to move on." At the time, I simply could not be that cavalier. Today, I know he was right. Does one have to dwell on bad experiences in order to heal from them properly? Or is it enough to acknowledge them, let dealing with the trauma make you a stronger person, and then move on? By the 1970s, I was getting deeper and deeper into psychoanalysis. I was undergoing medically guided LSD therapy, which had a tendency to put me in vivid touch with feelings and sense memories I didn't realize I had in my subconscious. One memory that stood out was of being a baby in the womb, listening to my mother and father argue about whether I should be aborted.

It was through this process that I remembered being left behind by my mother in South Carolina as a young girl. When I first realized that that event actually did happen to me, I felt the light come pouring in on my life as a woman. I also had abandonment issues from that lonely year in North Carolina during my childhood. I harangued my mother to death about it. And her only response was, "There was nothing else we could do at the time."

I would not let her off the hook. I needed to hold someone responsible.

But David was simply not invested in the culture of self-inspection that was taking me and California by storm at that time. He was warm, sophisticated, intelligent, driven, but relatively uncomplicated—unless you tried to deal with his schedule. Then it became very difficult. "This summer would you prefer a house in the Hamptons or elsewhere?" he asked. "We've been invited to spend time on the *Christina*. We should go!" (The *Christina* is the yacht Aristotle Onassis had named after his daughter.) We'd hop flights between Los Angeles, London, and New York. Soon I found myself making too much of the difficulties of life with a very positive man in constant motion. It was an easy way to stoke my old insecurities. "You know you don't deserve this man," a little voice in my head told me as David lavished me with love and attention. "He's too good to be true. If you open your heart to him, you'll have it broken."

He was always thinking about us as a couple, and worrying about my daughter. But each time we were apart, my raging insecurities and abandonment issues took over. They became criticisms. If he asked me to leave Las Vegas (where I was rehearsing) for an evening in New York because he needed me to give him my opinion on a new comedy act he was breaking in, I told him he was being unreasonable, forgetting all the times he jumped to help me. I sabotaged our relationship, finding problems anywhere I could. If he had to go off to report about the conflicts in Ireland, I ended up thinking he was having an affair while he was there. It was as if I needed to be the betrayed martyr. There was one awful night when I became ill at a party and he didn't leave with me quickly enough. I yelled that he was more concerned with networking than with me. He hated scenes. Frankly, I do, too. But I had to keep finding fault. If he thought I should travel when I didn't feel like it, I judged him harshly for it. When he tried to show me a house he wanted to buy for us in the English countryside (because I had admired a similar one not long before), I told him I was too tired to deal with such a thing. He was actually trying to tell me he wanted us to live together more formally, as a real domestic couple. Instead, I just found fault. I was simply a royal pain in the ass!

In 1972, while David and I were still supposedly a couple, I was working in Vegas when I met a man named Freddie Glusman. He owned women's shops at some local hotels, and was the polar opposite of David in every way. He had a raspy voice, and a jagged face that looked dangerous. He loved diamond wristwatches, gold rings, gold chains around his neck.

We had met in my dressing room after a show. The next day, large bouquets arrived. There were also boxes of clothes from his shops.

Despite myself, there was an animal attraction I felt to this very demonstrative man.

We had lunch, we had dinner. I was vulnerable and he was one of those men who knows how to take care of a busy woman in show business. He was always there for me. And while I knew life with David would be a constant challenge to improve myself, it was all so easy with Freddie. The only thing I needed to do for him was show up and look pretty. I knew that with Freddie, I'd call all the shots, and it was awfully nice to be the one in control. Freddie was no fool. He knew I thought he was garish. (I'm not sure what you'd call the gown I was wearing with my over-the-top Vegas spectacles at the time, but never mind.)

"Do you have to wear forty-two gold chains around your neck," I would ask him. "Please, at least button your shirt so we can get through dinner without making the table look like a hot tub." And, "Must you wear shirts that belong on a rumba band?"

"I know they don't dress this way in New York," he'd say. "But does everybody you're with have to walk around in Brooks Brothers blazers?"

It went on like that for quite a while.

"You're not going to wear those green alligator shoes to dinner, are you?"

"They match my green Piaget watch!"

Why the hell didn't I just get the hell out of there? Freddy had a big heart and he loved and adored my daughter and my mother, which touched me deeply. That had a great deal to do with why I remained.

That summer, I had returned to my apartment in New York after shooting a television special with Charles Aznavour, Twiggy, Louis Jourdan, and Perry Como. David and I had a fight at the Plaza over dinner. He had been toasting my success, saying "Here's to your show," and "Here's to us," and carrying on and on in his typically effusive way. I was seriously confused about what was going on with Freddie, and I really wanted to talk. So when he raised his glass for yet another toast, I smashed my glass into his. I was as stunned as he was. We decided to let our relationship cool. Meanwhile, I was keeping things going with Freddie. I felt like a hard-core two-timer.

One night David called and said he wanted to talk. At dinner at the Regency, he was not his usual buoyant self. "Darling, I have something to say to you," he told me in a highly theatrical manner. "I know there are differences between us, but I don't want to discuss them—they're not all that substantial. I also don't want to pressure you. But in my jacket I have two boxes. One contains a brooch. The other, a ring that you once admired in Asprey's in London. If you accept the brooch, we will continue our friendship. If you accept the ring, which I hope you will, then we will be engaged. Which will it be?" He put them on the table. He looked flushed in the dim light. And I was too stunned to answer. During the course of the evening, I told him I would love to accept his ring, but I needed his understanding and patience as I thought hard about the prospect of marriage.

I knew that with his travel schedule I'd end up at his side all the time rather than face being alone. So sooner or later, there would have to be major compromises in my life, and I was worried I'd resent him for it. He also wanted children. I had a daughter, and was already uncomfortable about not being with her enough because of my career, and I really didn't want the responsibility of another child. On the other hand, I loved David and I wanted to make him happy. We really were well suited to each other.

So we became engaged, and one day we came down to the lobby of the Plaza hotel, where we had a small apartment, and found hundreds of paparazzi and television networks snapping pictures of us and wishing us congratulations.

We had a lavish engagement party. We had a great time. But soon enough, he had to jet off to London or Australia or somewhere a lot farther than Vegas. I stayed in our apartment at the Plaza. I used to love living there, when I was earning my keep performing at the Persian Room. This was different. I was now simply the lady with David Frost.

We'd have good times when he returned, especially over holidays at my California home in Benedict Canyon. He was wonderful, swimming and playing pool with Suzanne, so much fun.

But each time he'd have to go away, I became more and more resentful.

Finally I phoned him and said I wanted to call it off for good.

He was shocked, but there was nothing he could do.

As had been the case with Monte Kay, I couldn't make it

work with a man who was secure with himself and only wanted what was best for me. A week or two later, I was back working in Vegas, and Freddie was right at my side, taking care of me while we went to dinner or relaxed on the boat he kept on Lake Mead. "You two look pretty comfortable together," one of his friends said.

"Well, I'm in love," Freddie said.

"So why don't you stop playing around and get married," the friend asked.

"Because she won't marry me."

Then I heard these words come out of my mouth: "I'm not so sure about that."

"So, do you want to marry me?" he asked.

"I guess so. Why not," I replied.

He gave me the biggest diamond ring I'd ever seen, and I told myself he'd take care of me forever and I'd never have to worry about being alone again. David called to be sure it was for real, and when I told him it was, he wished me every happiness.

In February 1973, I was whisked off to a wedding dinner to become a wife again. I was marrying Freddie without a word to thirteen-year-old Suzanne, who was attending the Athenian School in the San Francisco Bay Area. For that level of thoughtlessness, I have no explanation. I called my mother, who told Suzanne the news.

I moved through the next few months with hardly a thought in my head. And at first, I didn't take it seriously when Freddie became jealous of some of the men with whom I worked. Then his accusations grew more heated, especially about my working relationship with my record producer. One night in Lake Tahoe, I arrived back in our hotel room after a long and difficult day. Freddie was feeling amorous. I explained I was tired. That's when he started cursing at me and hitting me. I had heard he could be this way, but I had never seen it before. But suddenly the nice, fun guy had turned into a raging bully I didn't know at all. I locked the door behind me in the bathroom. Freddie tried to break it down. Security came in and asked him to leave the hotel.

He filed papers for divorce the next day in Reno. Then he called me to try to reconcile. I told him the marriage had never made any sense in the first place.

I never saw him again, and things were over with David, too.

I had hurt both men very badly. And I'd hurt myself.

To make matters worse, my career wasn't going anywhere. When *Julia* ended, I was not inundated with scripts. The show had run its course after three great years, and ratings were down enough that it was a good time to sign off. But to do what? I had to stick to what I did best, and there were television specials.

Then, in 1974, a role came along in an independent movie called *Claudine*. I played a welfare mother in Harlem opposite James Earl Jones as a sanitation man. It was a totally liberating and gratifying experience. I loved the character who inhabited the gritty world Julia had assiduously avoided. My performance earned me a 1975 Oscar nomination. One of the journalists who came to interview me at the time was a managing editor of *Jet* magazine named Robert DeLeon. He was a brilliant young man who at the age of fifteen had attended Moorhouse College on a full scholarship. I later learned he also had a daughter.

I met Robert again in Chicago, where I was performing at the Palmer House. He approached me after a press conference to ask if I would agree to have him cover my activities the day of the Academy Awards for his publication. When the day came, he presented me with a bracelet. It was an awkward, presumptuous gesture for a journalist covering a story. And when it was time to leave Los Angeles (I was disappointed after not winning the Oscar) to return to my singing engagement in Chicago, Robert had booked himself onto my flight in the seat next to mine. Who was this impetuous and very young man anyway, and what did he think he was doing?

On the plane, he made it a point to mention, during our effortless conversation, that he had separated from his wife. In Chicago the next night, he asked me to dinner. The evening started off badly. He was very rude to the maître d' when we had to wait for our table. Then he verbally abused a waiter. I told him he'd better calm down, and when he did, it became clear to me that he really was an exceptional young man. He was very ambitious, and a Fulbright scholar, which I particularly responded to because I still had issues around not graduating from college. He had a great position at Johnson Publications and a great future. We spent a couple of weeks seeing each other, and when he invited me to join him at a friend's house in St. Thomas, I thought it sounded fun. When I heard him tell his boss on the phone from the house in St. Thomas, "Guess who I'm with?" I became suspicious, realized I was being used, and that Robert was not the way he had presented himself. I didn't want to believe that, however. When he opened his suitcase and I saw he had packed almost nothing, and I volunteered to lend him some money to buy some clothes, I didn't think twice about that, either. I should have.

Once again, I found myself accepting everything and anything from a man who showed interest. Well, we had fun together. It didn't matter to me at the time that he was twenty-four and I was forty. In fact, older women and younger men were a bit of a feminist trend at the moment. But strangely, it was the camaraderie I enjoyed with him. Robert could talk about anything, and talk he did, first and foremost about marriage. And even though I'd been in therapy long enough to know it was okay for me to take charge around men, I let him arrange the wedding at Columbia University. It included exclusive coverage in *Jet,* unbeknownst to me. It wasn't until I saw our pictures on the cover months later that I found out about it.

Not long after that, Robert left his job at the magazine in Chicago and became a management consultant in Oakland. And what did I do? I left show business to follow right behind him and become a full-time housewife.

It was career suicide, but I enjoyed being a wife, at least for a while.

The trouble began with money. Robert had a modest income but expensive taste. And I found myself paying for everything—the luxurious home in Oakland (I sold my mansion in Beverly Hills to be in Oakland!), the Ferrari, the gorgeous clothes.

"You have to live in a certain style," he said.

My credit cards were flying and I just let it happen.

Then the drinking started. One night he was arrested for drunk driving, and I had to answer questions at an Oakland police station to keep an item out of the newspapers. Nine months after moving to Oakland for his new job, Robert quit. He wanted to get into public relations in Los Angeles. I said it was fine with me, but nothing more. "You know I don't have enough money to put an office together," he barked. "Why are you making me come to you and ask you for help?" So I told him I would back him until he was on his feet. He was foolishly optimistic, thinking he could just pick up the phone and have celebrities leave their press agents to be the clients of someone young and untested. "I'm really sorry, Robert, I can't do that," Sammy Davis had to tell him. "And for what it's worth, I think you ought to do everything you can to form this business on your own. Don't become Mr. Diahann Carroll." It couldn't be avoided. When Quincy Jones also turned him down, Robert resorted to his last hope—me—and pressured me to become his client. He'd be a press office with a client list of one.

"For the sake of your dignity, the people in this town have to know you're your own man," I told him. "I won't have anything to do with this."

Eventually, I suggested I live in New York for a period while he continued living in Los Angeles. As the time came for the temporary separation, Robert grew despondent. He'd been drinking for days when he said to me, "You're always going to be all right, aren't you?" I asked him what he meant. "I mean,"

he said, "you're always going to land on your feet, aren't you?"
I told him I hoped so and asked if that was a problem. "No,"
he said. "I just didn't know that about you. You will never
fail."

I went off to a rehearsal and he did not get home that night
at all.

It turned out that Robert had been speeding on Mulhol-
land Drive and lost control of the car. High above Los Angeles
on a winding road, he had tumbled to his death.

I was stunned. And I didn't know what to think, except
that perhaps for the first time in a long time, Robert, who had
been so young and tormented, was finally at peace.

I put on black and isolated myself from the world. Vodka
and wine helped. I couldn't seem to get a grip for months.
Friends could not rouse me. Robert's things were everywhere.
His date book was on his desk, opened. His toothbrush and ra-
zors were in the bathroom. Everything in my house reminded
me of the tortured young man who had been my third husband.

It was my mother who finally got through to me. "There's
nothing you can do for Robert anymore," she told me. "You're
still a young woman with a lifetime ahead of you. This isn't doing anyone any good, Diahann." And just like when I was a girl,
I listened to her. She was right. I slowly did get back on my feet,
just the way Robert said I always would. The Huntington Hart-
ford Theater had called my agent. Carol Burnett and Dick Van
Dyke were stepping out of a production of *Same Time Next Year*
and I was wanted by producers to step into the show to play

opposite Cleavon Little. I put everything I had into that role, my fullest concentration, and it ended up saving my life.

But I have asked myself if it was work that destroyed my marriage to Vic Damone twenty years later—or the fact that for most women, the combination of financial success and the glamour of Hollywood are too combustible a cocktail for most any marriage.

Vic did not want me to go away to Toronto for a year to be in *Sunset Boulevard*. When it became clear that I might actually get the part, we were visiting friends of his in Florida. This packet of music arrived, and I was playing a recording and singing to it one day, and Vic said, "These are very challenging songs vocally, and you're going to be away for a long time. I don't think you should do this." It stopped me cold. I put the music away. But I didn't respond. I certainly wasn't ready to tell him that it looked like I would be offered the part. I knew he didn't want me away from our marriage. And I'm still not positive in my heart that I didn't feel like a criminal for wanting the role. He never quite said, "Do you want this marriage or do you want your career?" But we were certainly in the realm of that kind of question. So it was there in the living room of his friends in a pleasant golf community in Florida that this deep emotional crevice had become even bigger between us.

Things had not been so peachy in our marriage, anyway. I knew that. We were comfortable on some levels, yes, and looked

Top: Dad, me, Mom, Sylvie, and the O'Gilvie family in 1945, at Lake Drew resort in upstate New York.

Left: Definitely counting on the legs, as I did not yet have access to couture. London, 1957.
HULTON/DEUTSCH COLLECTION/
CORBIS

Left: With friends at a fund-raiser at the Audubon Ballroom in New York—looking rather at ease even though I was half undressed. My father did not care for the costume.

Below: With my parents and my first husband at an anniversary party at my parents' home.

Above: Absolutely nothing exceeded the experience of working with the "Chairman of the Board," Frank Sinatra. Through his caring interaction with my four-year-old daughter, I was privileged to see the private side of him. BETTMAN/CORBIS

Left: My daughter, Suzanne, trying to protect our privacy on Fire Island in a 1967 photo shoot for a magazine. The fur was just a bit over the top. © ADGER COWAN

Clockwise from top: Husband number four, Vic Damone, and I enjoyed attending red carpet events together—both of us peacocks. TIME/ LIFE PICTURES/GETTY. Husband number two, Freddie Glusman, at our Hotel Bel-Air wedding in 1974. We basically walked down the aisle and in opposite directions. My friend Bob Goulet and me at the 22nd Tony Awards afterparty at Sardi's. © RON GALELLA/WIRE IMAGE. The genius behind Motown, Berry Gordy, at a Shirley Chisholm presidential fund-raiser at my Beverly Hills home.

Right: With Duke Ellington and Louis Armstrong in Paris during the shooting of the film *Paris Blues*. Duke treated me beautifully and decided to educate me in the finesse of dining on caviar. © HERMAN LEONARD PHOTOGRAPHY LLC/ CTSIMAGES.COM

Left: Paul Newman, me, Adele Ritt, and Kirk Douglas on the set of *Paris Blues*. © DELTA/PIX INC./ TIME LIFE PICTURES/GETTY IMAGES

Below: The cast of *Hurry Sundown*. Faye Dunaway, John Phillip Law, me, Robert Hooks, Jane Fonda, and Michael Caine. We were all thrilled to be on holiday in New Orleans.

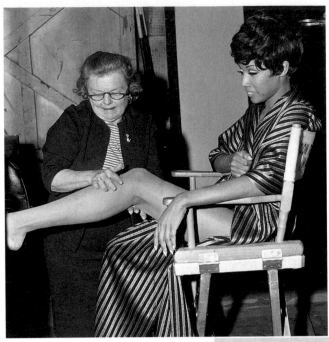

Above: Being made up on the set of *The Split*, in 1968. Gene Hackman, Donald Sutherland, and Jim Brown were costars. The plot left no public impression. I hope the legs did.

Right: Circa 1960s—my favorite backstage postshow attire in the Persian Room at the Plaza Hotel. *Harper's Bazaar* chose to use this look in a fashion spread.

Left: Sugar Ray Robinson and Diana Sands guest star on *Julia.* © BETTMAN/ CORBIS

Right: Me and my television son, Marc Copage, from the groundbreaking show *Julia.* Tumultuous times for both of us, and he was only five years old. © JOHN ENGSTEAD

Left: With the charming Maurice Chevalier in the 1967 French-American television collaboration "C'est la Vie." © AMERICAN BROADCASTING COMPANIES, INC.

Clockwise from top: Bob Hope visits the set of *Julia.* I was always receptive to his counsel. Presenting Zero Mostel with the Cue Magazine Entertainer of the Year Award in 1963 for his performance in *A Funny Thing Happened on the Way to the Forum.* I won the very first award the previous year for *No Strings.* © BETTMAN/ CORBIS. Me and JFK. If I only knew then what I know about him now. David Frost and me watching ourselves on different talk shows, a precursor to the new millennium of "TMI"— information overload. BILL RAY/TIME LIFE PICTURES/GETTY IMAGES

Clockwise from left: My second starring role on Broadway, created by Richard Rodgers, with my costar Richard Kiley. © RODGERS AND HAMMERSTEIN ORGANIZATION. Starring as Norma Desmond in the Toronto production of Sir Andrew Lloyd Webber's *Sunset Boulevard.* © CATHERINE ASHMORE. Ingrid Bergman, Natalie Wood, Jane Fonda, me, and Rosalind Russell rehearsing for the 1969 Academy Awards—the director has our complete attention. © RON GALELLA FOR WIRE IMAGES. Working with the brilliant Geraldine Page in the Broadway production of *Agnes of God,* the first time a black actress had ever replaced a white actress.

Left: Work hard, play hard—on my rental yacht: my musical director and great pal Lee Norris; the one and only Louise Adamo, who literally ran my life for over thirty years; and my personal manager and spark plug Roy Gerber, such a joy to be with—our working relationship lasted more than twenty-five years.

Below, right: As one of the Delany sisters at around a hundred years old. Not my best look. To get it, I spent three hours in makeup every day. A long time, even for me.

Above, left: Deep sea fishing, which I adore—this time off the coast of Hawaii.
Below: On the set of *Dynasty*. Big shoulders, hair, and boobs were on parade while gracious John Forsythe proposed a toast, reminding everyone that I had once been nominated for an Academy Award as best actress. © CBS STUDIOS

Above: Introducing my jewelry line, before the days of eBay.

Right: The American Syndication TV Press Tour in 1994; finally learning the versatility of denim jeans. TAMMIE ARROYO/GETTY IMAGES

Below: Brian, Jeffrey, and me celebrating my new eyewear line for B. Robinson.

Clockwise from top: Television's first black bitch, Dominique Deveraux, on the TV series *Dynasty.* I loved every minute of it! In the 1970s in my beaded Norman Norell sweater dress. Zip it up and no jewelry was necessary. It now resides at the Costume Institute of the Metropolitan Museum of Art in New York City. © MILTON H. GREENE, © RENEWED 2008 JOSHUA GREENE. My favorite of the four or five of my *TV Guide* covers. © MARIO CASILLI. Joan Collins gave me a bridal shower in 1986. When I walked in we both laughed at the similarity of our dresses. On *Dynasty,* this never would have happened.

Above: After the death of his second wife, I encouraged Dad to come visit Mom in Los Angeles after many years of estrangement. Her health was failing. But not her love for him.

Below: My mother's funeral in 2000 with Dad and my sister, Lydia.

Clockwise from top left: With my friends Selbra Hayes and Roscoe Lee Browne just before Roscoe left to visit Laurence Fishburne during *The Matrix* in 2003. Roscoe had a commanding delivery that captivated everyone, including my little grandson. The 30th annual Vision Awards to Fight Blindness gala in 2003. FRAZER HARRISON/GETTY IMAGES. Award presenters Carlos Santana and me at the 34th NAACP Image Awards in 2003. KEVIN WINTER/ GETTY IMAGE. With Harry Belafonte at my opening at Feinstein's at the Regency. It was my first intimate venue since my early years in the business. It was wonderful to be supported by my old friend.

Clockwise from top left: With Dionne Warwick at Feinstein's. Clearly this was not the moment I wake up before I put on my makeup. I was in high cover-up mode because my face was bloated from a cortisone shot I took for laryngitis. You do what you have to do in my business. With Angela Bassett. When she first moved to Hollywood we shared the same beauty salon. I watched her develop herself into a beautiful and sensual star. Backstage at the Regency with Tony Bennett, who I think is the greatest popular singer we have. He understands the discipline and the passion that is necessary to perform. We look pretty good at our age. With Vernon Jordan, who is one of the most naturally elegant, charismatic men I've ever met.

Holding my grandson! Overwhelmed by the feeling of holding my child's child.

like quite a happy and successful couple. But if things were so great, why did I always seem to need a drink around him? For years, I had stayed away from the drinking that was almost mandatory (Dean Martin and Frank Sinatra were my big show-business brothers, for goodness' sake!) in my field. And I was never fond of how my mother behaved after a couple of drinks. But with each man and each marriage, it is true that I found myself needing a glass of wine or a cocktail to accompany every bumpy conversation. With Vic, the drinking had gotten as close to dangerous as it ever had. I still remember the night we were out to dinner with some friends of his who didn't thrill me. But he wouldn't take my cue at the end of the night that I wanted to go home and do my exercises and go to bed. I should have just called a cab. But I was tipsy enough to get down on the floor and to start doing my exercises right there at the restaurant table. It may seem funny now, but at the time it was a sign that something was going very wrong between us.

Well, the year before that little incident, something happened that I could never forget or forgive. It made drinking more appealing to me. And it definitely made me re-evaluate our marriage.

Before leaving town one day, Vic told me to give his financial adviser a call. He thought I should have dinner with him and his wife while he was away. So the adviser called and suggested a very good restaurant, and I said I'd be delighted. I liked his wife very much and was looking forward to seeing them. When I arrived at the restaurant, my heart went into my throat because I saw this man was sitting alone, waiting for me. I felt strange immediately. My impulse was to flee, but I didn't. I said hello and sat down at the table as if everything were fine.

"And where is your wife?" I asked.

"Oh, she's not feeling well," he said.

"That's a shame," I said. "I wish you had told me that so we could reschedule."

"No, no, this is fine," he said.

There was something about his manner that got my antenna up very quickly. He was overly solicitous and made me so uncomfortable that when he went to pour some wine, I turned over my glass.

"I don't care for any," I said.

"Oh, come on, don't be silly," he replied. "We're going to have a wonderful evening and it's a wonderful wine. Try some."

I said, "You know, I really don't want any wine. No, thank you."

He continued to be obnoxious in ways that made me even more uncomfortable. Finally I got up and said I was leaving and told him good night. I was shocked to find he was following me to the parking lot. And when I opened the door to my car, he forced his way in beside me.

As I struggled, I screamed, "Please get out! This is exactly why I'm getting the hell out of here! I think your inviting a married woman to a dinner when your wife isn't present is not only impolite, but it's wrong."

That's when he told me, "Listen, Vic knows all about this."

"What are you talking about?" I said.

"He's knows all about this, so you don't have to worry."

It was hard to take in exactly what he was implying—I didn't actually think it was possible that my husband knew this would be happening. I mean how could any husband understand behavior so blatantly inappropriate—that a business associate would treat his wife in such an aggressive and shameless manner. But in spite of my continuing to struggle with him, he remained in the car—trying to impose his will upon me. He even smiled and told me how he'd always liked my looks. It was so insulting and embarrassing. I told him, "Get out now," and tried to push him out of the car, and he held on to my arm and laughed. That's when I scratched his face. I wanted to leave a mark on it that he would have to explain to his wife.

Vic was back from his trip, as I recall, when I got home. I walked into the house feeling dead because I was afraid to feel anything. I told Vic I had gone to dinner, and his friend had not brought his wife, and I didn't understand why that happened.

Vic's response was strangely flat and devoid of emotion.

"You should not have gone," he said. "Why did you go?"

"Because you told me to go."

"You didn't have to go, and when you got there, why didn't you leave?"

"But I did leave almost immediately."

He just shrugged and said, "Well, the only thing I can think is that you shouldn't have gone."

This wasn't the kind of reaction I expected from Vic. I had expected a completely outraged response. He was an old-fashioned husband in so many ways. Yet he wasn't understanding of my anger and confusion. It seemed very strange. So there was this silence. It was the kind of silence you have when ugly things are about to be said, and once they are, everything will change. So we didn't discuss it further. I had a drink or two and we quietly went to bed.

But that night I was so confused I could barely sleep.

A few weeks later, Vic and I were going to a country club for dinner and I told him I hoped we wouldn't be seated with the financial adviser and his wife. Vic told me I was a pain in the neck, but called ahead to arrange that we be seated at another table with our guests. And when we arrived at the dinner, the host met us and took me aside. He said, "I understand you did not want to sit at that man's table and I'm very sorry about that. But you are not the first woman in this club who has had to put up with that. And we really are going to have to do something about it." I told him to speak to Vic if he wished, but that's all I would have to do with it and I wouldn't say anything to anyone about it. At the end of dinner, the financial adviser approached with his wife to say hello. I did not see the scratches I had left on his face. But I knew from the look on the face of his wife that she knew something had happened. She couldn't look at me at all.

I've since observed that what felt like an isolated, and certainly isolating, event is not so singular in the business. We all know about the "casting couch" and the situations some women find themselves in when trying to break in. But little is said about what happens on the other end of the spectrum—once a woman has made it. The hustling kind of men, and there are many who succeed in Los Angeles, cannot help but see beautiful women as prey, women as commodities. They feed off of a woman's success. The money is easy and the lifestyle can seem fairy-tale-like; it's certainly more fun than a nine-to-five job for a man who has not found the kind of nine-to-five career that inspires him. But most women in my field cannot bring themselves to talk about it. I know women who've had to go through what I went through—and it's still happening today. In fact, despite my many marriages, it surprises me that young women still come to ask me for advice about love and marriage. My advice, these days, is pretty simple. You can love 'em but you don't have to marry them. After all, when and if it falls apart, the men almost always walk away without any repercussions.

It's a perspective I've acquired over time, but when that incident with Vic happened I didn't see it in such terms. I only knew that something between the two of us had unraveled. But like I keep saying, I'm really very foolish around men, and if there was some discomfort, I'd have a drink and try to forget about it.

But in some ways, I never forgot about it—to me it was tantamount to mental abuse by my husband. We had reached the lowest depth, one from which no marriage survives intact, because all trust and moral decency had been eliminated.

Several years later, when I was learning that *Sunset Boulevard* was going to take me to Toronto for a year, and that Vic really didn't want me to go, I found myself totally ignoring his wishes. My careerist mentality, the one that didn't make it possible for me to just say "okay, dear" started to bubble up. I was torn, but not as torn as I might have been had he been a better husband. And if my view of him had changed forever—on account of the incident with the financial adviser—Vic's view of me changed forever when I told him I would not turn down a year's contract to work in Canada.

It was too much for his macho mind to handle. What would he tell his Palm Springs friends when they asked, "Where is your wife?"

"Diahann's on the road, doing *Sunset*?"

It was self-centered of me to assume everyone was happy for me. But it was a part I'd been wanting to play for a long time, and it was coming at a time when I never thought anything like it would come to me again. As importantly, it would be another historic first—I'd be the first black actress to play the role. Okay, I'd already played a black bitch on *Dynasty,* but this was a deluded bitch of the silver screen in a spectacular production. The chance to do it was an enormous gift. But to Vic, it was a problem. I remember friends telling me to be careful. He was the kind of man who did not want to hear his wife get more applause than he did, ever, and I always had to be aware of that.

Perhaps that's why he didn't come to see me in Toronto very often. But one time, one of his good friends actually suggested that the billboards of me that were all over the city, on tops of buildings and sides of buses, be taken down before he showed up. That way when he arrived, he wouldn't see pictures of me everywhere.

It made no difference that this was not the Broadway, Los Angeles, or London production. He didn't want to see that his wife had become the Queen of Toronto.

What could make a man so unsupportive? Well, I've never been a popular Italian male singer. But I do know it's a heavy load, a responsibility to carry on one's shoulders because your musicality and masculinity and everything else about the way you carry yourself is involved in your work, even more than it is for a woman who wears tight dresses and high heels. I'd seen Vic's fans when I'd been on tour with him. Their devotion meant something to him. I'll never forget the time I was performing with him (once again, this was in Vegas) and I'd heard that one of his most devoted fans, let's call her Gloria, was in the audience. She had sent a note or something. Now, I'd heard about Gloria since I met Vic. She was at almost every show, but he only met her once, years ago, and since then she had always kept herself hidden from him a few rows back. One night the boys in the band were going on as they always did about Gloria being out there. I said, "Am I ever going to meet her? She's like some kind of mysterious legend." I went onstage to do my songs before Vic, and in the middle of my act, I said, "Stop the music! Ladies and gentlemen, we are honored to have a wonderful woman in the audience tonight who has been a fan of my husband's for twenty-five years. She is so loyal and so kind, and I think we should have her stand up so we can thank her for being that kind of fan! I want you to know how much I appreciate it, Gloria, and Vic does, too. Would you please stand up?"

And a spotlight turned to the audience and this woman stood up who was huge. Absolutely huge. I think the image Vic had in his mind all those years was that this devoted fan was still the cute, svelte young thing he'd met twenty-five years earlier. I know I had had the impression she would look like Jane Powell. Anyway, I didn't miss a beat. When Gloria stood up in all her glory, I walked off the stage to shake her hand and thank her.

But I do think I had burst a little bubble that night. Cavalier as show-business men of his generation could be, they really did have thin skin and big egos, and to find out that his biggest fan was literally his *biggest* fan must have been a little hard for Vic to take. I can still remember being on Dean Martin's show in 1965 with a group of Vic's peers. I was in a ball gown with hair reaching toward heaven, and they were all in tuxedos, holding cocktails and cigarettes, right on the air, mind you. Old times! Who was on? Dean, Frank Sinatra, Joey Bishop, Danny Thomas, yours truly, and about six cocktail waitresses being ogled and teased. Clearly, these men felt it was their obligation to joke about women as second-class citizens. But as I grew to know them, I figured out how smart they were, and how decent they were. They were just putting on an act. So when they'd pat my rear, I'd just pat theirs right back. They really were a bunch of adorable boys, who only pretended to be relaxed, when they were actually very focused and hardworking. We were like pals as we went around from one television variety show to the next.

The only time there was any tension with them was when we were all taping a Frank Sinatra special. Frank had just received word that Mia Farrow would not be returning home to him because she had been offered a role in the film *Rosemary's Baby*. We stopped shooting the show then and there, and a bunch of limos quickly appeared in front of the studio and took us all to dinner in a restaurant that had been closed for us in Century City. Frank looked ready to kill. His wife was choosing a job over him?

I suppose some of that same thing was happening between Vic and me in the 1980s. And now that I think of it, it's
also likely that this friend who suggested I have my billboards
removed from all over Toronto had been privy to Vic's reaction
from a previous visit.

"I really don't think I can get them to take any billboards
down," I told his friend.

I mean, can you imagine my telling the producer to do *less*
advertising? I can't say that being alone in Toronto for that year
made me realize how unsupportive Vic was. All I know is that I
wish we had both been able to speak our minds. He could have
told me directly to come home and I could have told him that
I could not leave the most important job of my senior years.
Then we could have had it out in a way that at least would allow
some real communication between us. Granted, I was not happy
at home—however, without realizing it, I re-created the exact
pattern of departure from my marriage that my mother had
created in her life.

Hard as it was to believe, Vic even started calling my drama
coach after seeing my performance. He asked her, "Aren't you
afraid of Diahann doing that role?" My drama coach, a very
feisty lady, asked him, "What are you talking about?"

He told her he thought it would give me thoughts of com-
mitting suicide.

She told him, "Hell no! Diahann would never do that!"

I thought it was interesting of him to think that. My character doesn't kill herself, she kills a man who disappoints her,
and at that time, I was more disappointed with Vic than with
myself. When I'd come to New York from Toronto on the nights

when the show was dark, I'd go to hear him singing at a midtown club where he was working. And I could not help but notice a little lady, who looked to be older than Vic, who had invited twenty guests to his show every night before taking them all to dinner in expensive restaurants. At first I did not take her seriously. But I could see she knew what he lived for—to be treated royally. It was enough that I helped him buy his Palm Springs house. Beyond that, I just wasn't comfortable supporting a man who was able to work and support himself. I wanted to keep things evenly split financially. But, as I'd learned, Vic was more ambitious about golf than about his career. And this little lady was, and still is, very rich, with several homes and her own plane. She knew what she wanted. Early on, she said to me, "I've been in love with him since I was fourteen years old, and I don't know how you could stand to be away from him for so long."

I told her, "Well, at this point, it ain't difficult."

One night she gave a small dinner party at her apartment. I was just back in New York after closing *Sunset*. When she was seating her guests, she said, "I want Vic to be at the head of my table!" I was shocked. We were still married. But I thought to myself that if she can be that rude, then she is probably very strong, and smart enough to know exactly how to make my husband very happy, and he's going to fall for it completely because she is very rich.

At the end of dinner, I told him I was going home alone.

I walked into the same apartment on Riverside Drive that I had decorated so zealously for Sidney, the husband who never materialized to live there with me so many years before. I could not keep from looking back and feeling like an absolute failure. Sure, I had just triumphed in Toronto. But my marriages had been nothing but disastrous, and a successful marriage was still stuck in my head, my old-fashioned, proper-girl head, as the ultimate goal.

Separation had become the only option. And I had some thinking to do. It took a long time, but little by little, over the course of months, I started to feel a change. I asked myself, "What are you going to do with yourself when you get up in the morning, Diahann? Is it possible to be comfortable putting your two feet soundly on the floor and saying, 'I'm single and I'm happy'? Because, my dear, there won't be any shoes under the bed other than your own! So why don't you try something new, and try living in a different way and keep the damn shoes away from the bed and see how it feels?"

And that's exactly what I did. It was not easy at first. But then it got easier and more pleasant. I found the majority of my time was spent with more interesting people who stimulated me and made me laugh. And we would do the kinds of things I liked doing, cultural things rather than singularly sports-related things, traveling to stimulating places rather than purely relaxing ones. And when I was at a party or dinner, I could look across a room and recognize the kind of person I'd want to talk to, and I would be able to talk to him or her without the burden of having to answer to someone on my arm.

There was no golf, and better yet, there was no jealousy or guilt or mind games.

And I thought to myself, "How wonderful that I can finally enjoy being alone!"

You know, ten years ago, I did not understand women who chose to be alone. But now, when I walk through my condo door after a lovely evening, it just feels marvelous. The other night I was coming back from an evening out, and as I was walking through my lobby—dressed to kill, I might add—a neighbor saw me and said, "Oh, don't you look wonderful, Diahann! We should have taken you with us!"

I didn't know what to say. Was she suggesting that I would have been happier going out with her and her husband than alone at dinner with my friends? There's an assumption in our society that a woman alone in a restaurant is lonely and that she needs a dinner partner, even if she has to rent one. I know women who do that.

It is a wonderful feeling to know your life is full just as it is.

That is not to say that I'm not open to relationships. I still have my beauty regimen before bed each night. I moisturize and brush my hair and enjoy my lovely lingerie.

It has taken some time to get to this present state of mind.

Some months after I left Vic with his lady in New York, I was back in Los Angeles, and I was still smarting from the loss of my marriage when I was sitting on the floor in the dark. I don't know why I had even bothered calling to tell Vic at that moment that I had just been diagnosed with breast cancer. I had already stressed him out with complaints about my injured leg from a fall I'd taken in *Sunset Boulevard*. I was, I guess, just a pain in the ass to him by that time. It just seemed that it was important health news to share with him, and I told him I didn't want him reading about it in the papers first. I wanted him to know that this was happening to me and that it was not necessarily serious.

His reply was shocking. "Oh, shit! What next, Diahann?" he said. Then he slammed down the phone. Wouldn't that make your knees crumble and put you on the floor? I was alone. I had cancer and I was out of work.

I think I knew that I'd eventually land on my feet.

But that night I was flat out on my ass.

FIVE

Sickness and Health

MALIBU WAS CALLING ME IN THE SPRING OF 1997. MY old friend Nigel (a charming actor whom I had met years ago through my mother) and I would go driving up the Pacific Coast Highway looking at summer rentals. I thought it would be a nice change to be by the ocean, find a place where Mom could visit with me and enjoy a vacation. There was one place that was just so airy, with a big open kitchen facing the ocean and a fireplace in the den, and I just imagined how relaxing it would be. She could be Malibu Mabel, I could let some clean sea air into my new life, and we could hold court on a balcony looking over the ocean.

But that plan was not meant to be because shortly thereafter, I received the news that there was a spot on my mammogram. It was nothing I could see, even with the doctor pointing it out to me, but before I knew it, I was having a biopsy. The results came back immediately.

"Good news and bad news," said Dr. Barry Rosenblum, a

very warm man and a good friend. "You do have cancer, but it is so early that the tumor is less than a centimeter in size, and we can be very happy about that."

I didn't panic when I heard the news. I do remember thinking, "But I have always taken such good care of myself, exercised and eaten well!" It was as if I'd paid my union dues and was expecting a pass for the rest of my life. I mean what gives one cancer? Who knows? Thin, nonsmoking nutrition nuts get it. It seems to me that other than smoking and genetics, you can't blame cancer on anything specific. It is too often blamed on stress. Stress! When I was a girl, we didn't know the word stress. Life is always fraught and difficult, and if it isn't, you aren't really alive. So I didn't look to blame my cancer on anything.

I looked exactly the same, yet suddenly everything was different. I had cancer. I had a new job to do, and that's when I pulled myself out of the initial stupor I felt after getting the news and became very businesslike, almost as if I were dealing with a problem with an orchestral arrangement.

"Might it be someplace else in my body?" I asked my doctor.

"We're just going to deal with this first," he said. "With cancer, you must take things step by step." He sounded a little off, a little sheepish.

"Is there anything else I should know?" I asked.

"Well, yes. I'm afraid I have to have my associate take care of you for the next two weeks. I promised my children we'd go away together in July, and I've already postponed once, and I just can't disappoint them again. It's too important."

"Barry," I told him, "you don't know how right you are!"

I meant it. I knew from personal experience the emotional costs of putting work before family. But I was also worried. I was fortunate to need only radiation. It would be a nine-week program, starting as soon as possible. Suddenly there was a lot to think about. I had to tell everyone. And my goodness, they had so much to tell me in return. The phone never stopped ringing with friends wanting to be helpful with information and connections. It was overwhelming, but also endearing and ultimately useful to me because I like as much information as possible. Only this bordered on overload. "This doctor is head of oncology! This doctor is my neighbor's brother and he's a genius!" I heard about alternative medicine, acupuncture, and naturopathic practitioners, the value of Sloan-Kettering in New York, meditation, diet, and God knows what else. It became a cacophony of opinions. One question kept coming up more than any other. "You're going to go to Cedars-Sinai, aren't you, Diahann? They have the best treatment in California! Plus it's five minutes from your house!" In fact, that's where I assumed I would have my radiation treatments. My doctors are all there and it's a great hospital, of course. But when I went in for a consultation, I realized it's just such a big impersonal place. There was also the possibility of running into all kinds of people whom I knew or who recognized me there, and that made me uneasy. Besides, I actually wanted a little distance between my home and my radiation treatments. I just thought it might be nice to have my treatments closer to the ocean, where the air and light is always fresher.

After much research, I found a much smaller institution, St. Johns Medical Center in Santa Monica. Friends were skeptical.

But I had to trust myself on this one. St. John's has a stellar reputation, with state-of-the-art cancer treatments, including the latest in radiation technology. Plus, when I got out of my car for my first appointment, I could feel the ocean air nearby. The air is very refreshing in Santa Monica. The staff was incredibly warm, the facility far less imposing in size, and the atmosphere was better for me in every way. So I knew I'd made the right choice. And I think that there are times when taking control based on your gut can be just as beneficial as doing what everyone tells you to do. The treatment was going to be part of my life for several months. Why not have it done at a place that I knew was excellent, but that was also more pleasant for me? Nigel said we could have lunch by the ocean after each treatment. That sounded wonderful!

So the first day, he drove me in my Rolls, right up to this hospital. And a young man in the radiation oncology department guided me in to look at the machine. It was the biggest machine, just huge. I had to take off my blouse and bra, and I was given a cotton bra to wear. The whole thing was not nearly as embarrassing as I thought it would be. Anyway, I wasn't about to show how scared I was. I felt it was better not to acknowledge my fear. In fact, I was rather jovial (to help cover up my tension) as I lay down on this black conveyor-belt-like thing that moved me into place. The young man administering the radiation could not have been more accommodating. I admired his skill at making small talk in order to keep me at ease. (Being with staff who are able to make light conversation can really make a difference in how you feel about a medical procedure.) Anyway, I liked this fellow very much. I was lying there under the radiation machine, as if in a cave, and not feeling a thing as it did its work, the thought inexplicably came to me that if a cure for cancer were found, then this young man and thousands of others would be out of work. Each year 140,000 women are diagnosed with breast cancer alone. My treatment took a half hour.

I had the most incredible team. The head of radiation oncology was Dr. Takita. I will always remember our talks. He explained to me that it's very hard for specialists to deal with cancer because it keeps changing, one strain transforming into another. But he also assured me that treatment has progressed so far in recent years that many people live with it as a chronic rather than a terminal illness. I cannot tell you how grateful I was to have a doctor who was so open to conversation and sharing information. When I was telling him about Vic's brusque reaction to my news, he told me how differently families deal with things in Japan. Beginning in his childhood, his parents had prepared him for life changes, not just love and marriage, but aging and illness, too. It's a good way of keeping you from wasting time, knowing you only have so many years to be young and foolish, and only so many years to be free of worries about your health as an adult. Dr. Takita was the first doctor to talk to me openly about menopause. None of my friends were prepared to talk about it. We can see it happening to one another, but don't want to put it into words. In America, people tend to run from illness and aging, rather than embracing them. But Dr. Takita and his team of therapists wanted to know how my family was reacting to my cancer. Did they see me as a whole person, not just a cancer patient?

Yet I couldn't help but feel contaminated, and I felt I didn't have the blessedly clean body I once had. Suddenly there was this virus, this germ in my body, that made me feel uncomfortable, unattractive, and out of control. So it helped that Dr. Takita and the therapists on his staff worked to help me overcome my insecurities. St. John's is very much geared for the cancer community, with all kinds of support programs for patients and their families, from diet consultants to group therapy. One of the most supportive things Dr. Takita did for me during my treatment time was tell me it was fine for me to have a glass of wine at lunch after I left radiation.

"You're kidding," I said. "Really?"

"You have to keep living," he said.

And that's what I did. My friends were amazing. They'd pick me up after my treatments and we'd go have lunch on the beach. I felt they were as important as the radiation at that time. I didn't want to involve my mother too much because she was pretty frail by then and I didn't want to upset her. I'd been performing on the road constantly for much of my life, so I've been lucky to have friends who understand that and who still would stand by me when I needed them most. Their intentions in helping me with cancer were just so loving and pure. As you get older, friends become more and more important. They can keep you alive—in fact, studies of the elderly have actually proven that seniors with a larger social network live longer and healthier lives. Nigel was so amazing. As were other friends who invited me to the theater, films, and dinner and made me feel more engaged than I'd felt in years. They acknowledged my fears about cancer, but also let me know we had to continue to enjoy one another.

One of my biggest caregivers was my friend Marilyn. Along with Nigel, she was such an important source of comfort. She waited with me at doctors' appointments that were a constant source of worry and tension. Mostly she offered the calm, caring companionship I needed to feel less alone with my illness. I was extremely lucky to have her and so many other friends around to buoy my spirits.

However, I was not so lucky to develop chicken pox in the middle of my radiation treatments. That's right, chicken pox! My mother verified that I had had mumps but not chicken pox as a child, and when you have radiation, your immune system is depressed. "God," I said, "I believe in testing people for endurance, and I've always been a hard worker all my life, but I think you're overdoing it here!" I really did feel overwhelmed. I mean chicken pox potentially all over my face and body while struggling with cancer? But even as I fussed and fumed, some voice inside of me said, "Oh, be quiet, Diahann. You're going to handle this. You don't have any choice." And so I did.

Radiation was postponed, and I went shopping. I mean, what else was there to do when a new wardrobe was required of me? Style matters, even when you have chicken pox! So I bought about a dozen big white shirts, men's shirts, because the spots had reached my hands, and I didn't want anyone to see them. Thankfully, the spots stopped at my neck and did not get onto my face. That would have been awful for someone as vain as I am. "Does this mean you're giving me a break, God?" I asked. As soon as I wasn't contagious, I'd go out to dinner again with friends.

I eventually went back to radiation. Connie Chung did a

segment about my cancer, following me right into treatment. I was thrilled to do this because the conversation Connie and I had was the kind women friends might have shared, but in this case it was for a national network audience of millions of women who were too intimidated to discuss their situations. But my manager, Brian, and others had helped me decide not to try to keep my illness a secret.

It sounds less of a big deal now than it was ten years ago. After all, when someone like Elizabeth Edwards spoke so honestly and openly in the middle of her husband's presidential-primary campaign, it is hard to imagine why anyone would keep it to herself. But I can tell you why it's easy to fall into secrecy. It's because you don't always want people asking how you are and reminding you of this frightening thing in your body. I like attention when I'm on the stage. When I'm having dinner or on the phone, I like a little more give-and-take. So it would have been easy to just bury the whole thing. On the other hand, I knew so little about my illness going into it that I thought it would be wonderful to get some more information out there to the general public. But there was and still is such a stigma about having cancer in Hollywood. Colleagues told me going public had a negative effect on their careers, and that it certainly didn't help them seem as attractive and desirable in a sexist industry. So it was a big deal for me to decide that I would give interviews and say, "Yes, I have breast cancer." And it was wonderful to receive calls later from women in the industry who told me they were facing the same challenge.

The thing is, I was lucky. I didn't need chemotherapy. They'd caught my cancer early, and I wasn't sick or incapacitated by my treatments. I didn't even have a sensation of burning while being radiated. Radiation today has become so sophisticated and precise that it impacts your life only minimally. Even chemotherapy has become more precisely calibrated, so although it still can be exhausting, some women don't even lose their hair. The radiation darkened a spot of my skin, but there was no pain. And my energy level remained high. So I had no trouble giving interviews.

I gave a number of interviews. And it turns out that being a spokesperson is a role I enjoy. And of course I had been wearing wigs for years, so when women undergoing chemotherapy needed some advice, who better than I to give it to them? Women had always related to me as a role model. Now I was looked up to for another reason. And getting out there to talk about my problem turned out to be as beneficial to me as it was to the people I was speaking to. I genuinely believe it was good for my health. I did interviews on radio and in newspapers. I signed on with various organizations, such as the American Cancer Society. One, called the Wellness Community, has created a network of facilities where people can drop in for information about the best way to deal with cancer, and with situations having to do with work, family, and expenses as well. Several times a year, I also address large groups of lower-income women from the black, Hispanic, and Asian communities.

I talk about my own experience, and about the need for prevention. The whole world of cancer needs demystifying, particularly in lower-income communities. Women are still intimidated. So while things are always improving in terms of the number of people getting mammograms, I still meet plenty of women who would never consider having one. They believe the machine is dangerous. By hearing me tell my own story, they come to view the process as much more accessible. It helps for them to see someone of color talk about these issues. These women need to hear from a ten-year survivor that mammograms are not dangerous and that without them, my cancer would have spread.

It can be quite shocking. I remember one day when two women approached me at the dais after a talk I gave in Houston. They wanted to know if I would go home with them to speak to their mother personally. She was refusing to have a mammogram. She believed that there was nothing available to help fight cancer anyway, so why bother? In fact, this lady told her daughters that it wasn't even possible that someone famous like me would be coming to town to discuss her cancer. I actually considered going with these girls and making a personal appearance at their mother's home. But I also wondered if crossing that kind of boundary was a good idea. You can always do more, I guess. But in the end, someone from my organization got involved. I was just glad I was in a position to help at all.

In another city, I was giving my talk and explaining that a mammogram truck would be coming in on Thursday. A woman came up to me and asked, "Does that mean for black women, too?" Another asked if Asian women were included. I was just stunned to hear from women who believed they would be turned away from testing because of the color of their skin or the language they spoke. It's all so enlightening. I would probably never have the opportunities to visit these communities, learning so much about our country, if I had not had cancer.

One day I was at a hotel in Chicago, where I was shooting *The Delany Sisters*. I was eating breakfast very early in the morning before going off to the set, when three young ladies on the staff of the hotel approached to thank me for a radio spot I'd done. After they had heard it, they vowed to go get their mammograms together, and two of the three discovered they had breast cancer early. There we were, at dawn, three strangers, sharing something so important, lifesaving really. We were all cancer-free.

It's ironic: I'd spent my life on the road, and just when things were slowing down in my professional life, I found it necessary to speak in public to share my cancer experience with others. I'm still performing, too, of course, concerts, nightclubs, and the like. I have to admit that at this stage of my life, it's a shot in the arm to know that hundreds and sometimes thousands of people want to come hear me.

It's been ten years since I had cancer, and they say that after seven or eight years you're pretty much in the clear. But I have never felt completely at ease. Each time I go for a mammogram, it makes me anxious, and when the appointment in my book tells me I have one on Thursday at 3 P.M., I am tense until the moment I hear "you're fine." I worry for those around me, too. Like Nigel, who had been so good to me when I was going through treatment (even as he was finding out that he had cancer himself). We sit together, alone or with Sharon, his friend, having drinks and holding hands. Often it is on my terrace around sunset, when the Hollywood Hills outside my window are glowing.

The other day he called and asked, "Is it the golden hour yet?"

He lives nearby, and knows he doesn't have to ask if it's convenient to come over. He knows he can just come. And so we sit, enjoying the magnificent view. Nigel is a gentleman, younger than me and Caribbean-born and -raised, with the most beautiful lilt in his voice that only adds to his charm and dignity. The only time we ever had an argument was when he was complaining about the hospital where he was going for his cancer treatment. I had never heard of it and made it my business to badger him until he changed hospitals. Now he's much more comfortable and confident that everything that can be done is being done. But we don't talk about our health all that much. We're enough at ease with each other to know we don't have to discuss it. It's a tribute to his character, I think, that Nigel has not become his illness, and continues to delight everyone he knows. If there's something he needs to share, he shares it. He still has his wicked humor. And he hasn't lost one ounce of his capacity to enjoy life.

We enjoy a glass of wine or a cocktail with tinkling ice in our glasses and warmest thoughts in our hearts. No doctor has told us we can't have our cocktails. So we're having a good time for now, no matter what the future may bring. One evening when I was feeling low—it was my birthday—he put on a Tony Bennett record in my living room and asked me, "May I have this dance?" It was as therapeutic as any treatment. When you are ill, friends are a very potent and necessary form of therapy.

Cocktails, indeed. Just as I'm reluctant to give up my high heels, I am not one to give up my cocktails. Besides, with the news today touting red wine as good for cholesterol counts, and doctors recommending that a couple of drinks a day may be more beneficial than detrimental to your health, perhaps they are just as healthful as the pomegranate juice I drink for its antioxidants. Who knows? But I do try to stay in good condition so that if anything goes wrong again, I'll be strong enough to fight it. The stronger you are, the better shape you're in, the more chance you'll have of surviving whatever hits you in your senior years.

Since cancer, I also find that I am far more conscious of how I'm spending my days. What do I want to do? And with whom? I make more time for friends than I ever have before. Most importantly, I cherish every moment that I have with my grandchildren and their mother—my daughter, Suzanne. A few years ago, she was visiting me in Los Angeles on her birthday, when she told me she had not had her mammogram. Although she always wanted to make her own way in the world without my string pulling, she was happy that I suggested she could get to be seen right away at a private facility that I use. You're in and out of there quickly, and best of all, you get your results right away. So I went with her and sat in the waiting room, and even as I delighted in reading books to my grandchildren and marveled at their excellent waiting-room manners, I worried intensely about what was going on inside with the exam. This was, after all, the place where I first got the news of my breast cancer. Would the doctor find something on my daughter's breast, and then ask to call another doctor? You always dread that. Fortunately, this was not necessary. Instead, the doctor came out to see me in the waiting room. And we hugged. Here I was in the very place where ten years before I had first heard the news of my own cancer, and I had to hold back some tears, but they were tears of joy.

SIX

My Best Girl

I'VE BEEN NOMINATED FOR OSCARS AND EMMY awards. And I've won a Tony and a Golden Globe. But a nomination for Best Performance as a Mother was never even a remote possibility. I was always a hardworking woman and my daughter, Suzanne, always had to pay the price. These days, actresses often wisely take a break from their careers so that they can raise their children. But as one of the few consistently working blacks of my day in Hollywood and on Broadway, I was too caught up in the money and impact I was making to understand how important it is for a mother to put her child above all else.

I mean, can you imagine having Diahann Carroll as your mother? My daughter, Suzanne, had to share me with a very demanding career, and, as a little girl, watch me go off to work all over the country, leaving her with her nanny for half her childhood. To make matters more difficult for her, I've always been the kind of show-business person who tends to be "on" most of the time. It makes intimacy harder to achieve with an innocent and vulnerable child. But then, I've seen very few people of my generation in politics or show business who know how to drop the "on" persona, even in private. It's not that we know we're behaving that way. There's just a built-in tendency to charm any room, and get as much attention as possible, even though nobody's paying a dime for the show. Of course, when you spend as much time as I do preparing to look good in public, people do notice you. I suppose some children might have enjoyed it. Not Suzanne. But to her credit, she has gotten over any issues that built up over the years.

The primary cause of our reconciliation has come in the form of her children, my grandchildren. Nothing in my life has prepared me for the sheer joy of them and in watching Suzanne develop as a mom. She has shown herself to be a fantastic hands-on mother of two. Oh, the joy she elicits from her children! It reminds me of the laughs she and I had together when she was still very young. In our earliest days, there were many delicious moments. How could we not have them while traveling on the road together?

One of the stories I love to tell is about the time she used Frank Sinatra as a desk. In 1964, she would have been four years old. I had brought her to the set of *The Dean Martin Show,* which was not exactly a child-oriented situation, with all the smoking, foul language, carousing, and martini swigging that was needed to inspire the entertainment. Plus, shooting live television is never relaxed, but rather very intense, with as much hustle and bustle backstage as any Broadway show, if not more. Somehow I succeeded in making a deal with the producers that Suzanne could be there as long as she was quiet.

She was quiet. But that didn't mean she would sit still. She was much too sociable a child for that. She was unafraid, and felt it was her right to engage anyone on hand in coloring with her crayons. I was backstage listening to something Dean was singing, and Suzanne quietly left my side to walk over to Sinatra, who was sitting in a chair, being quiet as well. He was wearing a suit and tie and hat, as I recall. Suzanne didn't care that this man was not dressed for arts-and-crafts time. Nor did she care that he was one of the nation's greatest celebrities. In her most methodical manner, she quietly uncrossed his legs and put her coloring book on his lap. Then she walked back over to me to get her crayons. He didn't move, and when she returned to him, she started to color, very intently and quietly. He never moved. She kept coloring. Eventually, the whole room became aware of it happening, and I was about to leap up and rescue him.

He put his hands to his lips to indicate he didn't want me to disturb her.

I, of course, loved him for that for the rest of his life.

And for Suzanne, it was just another take-your-daughter-to-work day.

She was used to it. For her first Christmas, she joined me in France for the filming of *Paris Blues*. Never mind that Sidney was to be my romantic interest. As I said, I simply could not say no to a film that was so intent on lending dignity to the conversation about race in America at the time. But for the first part of the shoot, Suzanne was too young to travel, and I missed her so much that I made a fuss at Orly Airport as soon as her plane landed. In those days, you could still greet arriving passengers at the gate. I stood with a crowd, trying to get a glimpse of her as I jumped up and down. She was with my parents and my husband Monte. It was taking a long time for them to get security clearance. I was frantic. "What is the matter, madam?" an attendant asked me.

"You don't understand," I shrieked. "That's my baby there!"

I was so unmoored that they ran ahead to bring her to me.

The entire family occupied a three-bedroom suite at the Hôtel de La Trémoille on that trip. My parents were very impressed, watching how unafraid I was to ask for anything on my child's behalf—in my very poor French, I might add. They had grown up in an era when African-Americans were made to feel they couldn't make any demands at all. So seeing their daughter behave as I did, so confident and unapologetic, made a big impression.

Suzanne, at age two, was on the road with me again in 1962. The entire company of *No Strings* was on a train headed to Detroit, for an out-of-town tryout. In those days, train travel was still relatively formal and fabulous, or at least it was for us. Suzanne had a nanny, Mary, and along with my assistant and entourage, we were quite a formidable group, with a beyond-formidable amount of luggage. I made sure we had lots of berths for all of us, and that my little daughter had full run of them. Imagine her delight. And when it was time for supper, Suzanne was all dressed up and looking so adorable that there wasn't a person in the dining car who didn't fall in love with her.

One evening, during cocktail hour, she was running around the parlor car in a perfect little red velvet dress. Richard Rodgers walked in, dressed impeccably, as always, in a well-cut dark suit, white shirt, and tie. He saw Suzanne and laughed, then picked her up and started talking to her and getting very involved. Who knows what those two were talking about. I couldn't hear over the sound of the train. But of course I was pleased and impressed. What young mother wouldn't be? In those days men had very little to do with children who weren't their own, and it was so lovely to see this rapport. But after a while, I had to interrupt to say, "I'm looking at the time and I think you should put her down now." Mr. Rodgers ignored me and sat down in a banquette to continue playing. "It's her bed-time, Mr. Rodgers," I repeated. "And I think you'd best put her down now."

He still ignored me. And that's when she peed in his lap.

Later, when we were rehearsing in New York, I was back-stage one day when I looked over and found my leading man, Richard Kiley, passing Suzanne around.

"Isn't she cute?" he was saying as he gave her to another cast member, who then gave her to another one. "Put your hand on her head."

I walked up to him and shot him a withering look.

"What are you doing?" I asked.

"Well, you know it's good luck to touch a colored baby's head, Diahann," he said.

I grabbed her away from him faster than you could say "Do you want to die?"

"Get your hands off my child," I said.

Poor Richard Kiley. He was so alarmed.

"What's the problem, Diahann?" he asked.

"That is unacceptable," I said. "Unless you're going to let me put my hand on a white child's head to bring me good luck because she's white, you can't do it to my child because she's black. Don't ever do that again!"

"I never heard it was unacceptable," he said.

"Well then, I'll be the first to tell you," I replied.

I do think that the exposure to the magical backstage world of show business taught Suzanne to be at ease in all kinds of situations. She became very comfortable anywhere we went, and could actually be very assertive. If she needed help coloring or tying her shoe, she'd enlist anyone who was handy. One time I sent for her when she was about five, while I was performing in Vegas. I was very worried while waiting for her at the train station. Imagine a time when there were no cell phones to keep nervous young mothers updated at every moment of a trip. When the train pulled in and people were disembarking at the Las Vegas depot, several looked at me, smiled wearily, and volunteered, "She's on the train!" She had made herself very well known. She stepped from the train in her little blue wool overcoat, looking ready for a visit to the White House. It felt like heaven having her there. When we arrived at my suite, she settled right in. She was accustomed to hotels, and immediately asked, "Is this my room?" We set up a suite for her as her play space, with a little table and chairs. And when there were other children around on set, we would invite them up to play school.

Wherever we went, we'd set up house for weeks at a time.

There would be a nanny, and sometimes my mother, and in later years a teacher. I'd come back from work tired and in need of resting my voice. She wanted my full attention. Thank heavens she enjoyed the company of Louise Adamo, my assistant for over thirty years, whose sense of humor and love of children were obvious. Louise was a happy addition to our family. But Suzanne still had to spend a great deal of lonely time in hotels.

I remember one of Suzanne's last moments of true innocence while traveling with me, before things started to change between us.

We had started the national tour of *No Strings*. She was backstage in the wings during a run-through, and was two years old, old enough to understand that she was to stand still when I told her to. So there she stood (with my wardrobe mistress) watching me with her big eyes as I stepped into the spotlight and sang a number after which I'd return to her open arms in the wings. The day it all changed was when a stage manager who adored her (there wasn't anyone who didn't) made the mistake of picking her up and taking her from backstage to the front of the theater. There were producers and friends in the audience watching the rehearsal. She saw them, then she turned in the aisle to see me onstage in a spotlight and yelled at the top of her little lungs, "Wait! That's my mommy!" It was the first time she saw me as the performer on a stage, really. Who were all those strangers paying such rapt attention to her mother, the one person in the world who she thought was for her and her alone? After she yelled, the entire production buckled under with laughter. It took a long time for everyone to calm down.

And it took decades to undo the damage my career would

cause us in the years ahead. Of course it did not help that a year after her birth, I had asked her father for a divorce. Fortunately, he stayed firmly in her life, and was more of a rock to her than I could ever be. But it never occurred to me to allow her to live with him. In those days, a mother had to have her child with her.

When Suzanne reached school age, I enrolled her in the elite Lycée Français on the Upper East Side. This school was supported by the Kennedys. The curriculum was adapted for traveling families and the children of international businessmen and diplomats. I hired tutors who were recommended by the school. I'd receive reviews from the headmistress that my darling daughter was bright and always did well and seemed to enjoy her assignments.

But even as she succeeded with her schoolwork and was exposed to the exciting world of show business, I was concerned that being on the road was not the best thing for her. Eventually, the school confirmed my concerns. When she was seven, the headmistress called to tell me how hard it was for children to constantly be pulled away from school. They can't build relationships or bond with friends, and indeed, when Suzanne returned to school after being on the road with me, she was disoriented. Other children were forming alliances without her. It could be a nightmare for any child.

Not that it was all great when we were home. "Mommy, why don't you bake cookies?" Suzanne once asked me. I told her I wasn't that kind of mother. I was more eager to buy the best cookies in New York for her. I'd often return from rehearsals only to learn I'd missed suppertime and bath time, too. She doesn't remember that I read her stories at night whenever I could. But it wasn't enough and I knew it. At the Central Park Petting Zoo one afternoon, we were pursued by fans. Standing between me and them, she told them, "Please go away! This is *my* mommy."

Of course she was absolutely right. I should have learned to tell people, "I'm sorry, but this is family time." There's a photograph taken around that time, a fashion shoot for a magazine, since I was wearing a full-length fur coat on the beach in the middle of summer: mother and child are standing together at water's edge. The sea is behind us. My fake eyelashes are casting shadows on my cheekbones, and my hair is piled very high. I look absolutely preposterous, pretentious, and untouchable, fashion-model style. In front of me stands my little girl, age six or so, in a darling ruffled bikini. I have an imperious look on my face to rival that of Nefertiti. She is a little, long-haired, natural beauty of the kind that Gauguin might have painted. But the look in her eyes is not tranquil. She stands up against me protectively, as if she were trying to keep the camera away.

The worst possible thing for our relationship was to have to leave her at home. But my work called. In the mid-1960s, as I've said, I was part of a group of blacks who were breaking into the entertainment industry in new ways. Sammy Davis Jr., Harry Belafonte, Nat King Cole, Sidney Poitier, Lena Horne, Eartha Kitt—we were riding something wonderful and giving a guilty and conflicted nation what they wanted to see. So eight weeks in Tahoe or Vegas? Yes. Role in a sophisticated film? How could I say no? Guest appearance on *What's My Line?* or the

Steve Allen Show? What about flying to Hollywood for *The Danny Kaye Show, Hollwood Palace, Carol Burnett,* or any special that wanted me? Of course! It would have been too difficult not to accept the heady opportunities of that moment.

So more and more, Suzanne was left behind. I'd leave her in the care of a nanny, Monte, or my parents. And I truly thought they would smooth over my absence. But all these wonderful people were no substitute for her mother. So when she'd get home from school and find me preparing to hit the road and see my mountains of luggage in the foyer, she would break into tears and whimper that she hated luggage. It broke my heart.

Her time was always more pleasant with her father, I'm afraid. He was more easygoing, and at home for her more, and even while he was busy becoming a successful music and television producer, he loved to entertain guests who gave Suzanne the attention she craved. Monte preferred to spend time with her more than anyone or anything in his life. When she was a girl, they'd comb the beach or bookstores for hours together while trying to soothe the broken areas of our lives. Monte never discredited my ambition to our daughter. He was not a mean-spirited man. His was the pure, hopeful, and unselfish love that is necessary to build a family. We all felt it, but never spoke of it. There's no doubt that it was his love for her that sustained them both while she was growing up. Painful as it is to admit, he understood the needs of a child better than I did.

Well, every family has issues; at least all the interesting ones do. I had somehow created a competition between my daughter and my career, and my career was winning. Part of it was a simple quest for the material things that my parents had struggled to have. I wanted them for Suzanne, too—more languages, more travel, more opportunities to develop, the best of everything. I succeeded in providing her with a fabulous home and financial security. Her infant crib, from Saks Fifth Avenue, had been handcrafted. Her pram was shipped over from Harrods of London. When we moved to Los Angeles, it was in high style. But none of it helped a child who only wanted what she deserved—more of her mother.

It became particularly difficult when she was nine, and I'd become the popular television mother Julia. I was gone in the mornings before she left for school, and although I had built an elaborate playground for her on the grounds of our newly acquired, spectacular home, I couldn't play with her on weekends often because I was locked in my room memorizing lines. My life was in high gear and she was left in its wake. It was a surreal moment for me, all that unnatural attention at once. There was the man in prison who sent me a box filled with things belonging to a fellow inmate who had died . . . There was a thirteen-year-old boy who called to tell me I was his long-lost sister and his whole family was coming to visit us for Christmas. Eventually, I called studio security to intercept his calls.

Poor Suzanne had to contend with the little boy who played my son on *Julia*. Marc Copage was an adorable, chubby-cheeked, lisping five-year-old. His mother had left him when he was an infant. He followed me around the set as if I were his real mother. The scenes we had together were incredibly playful. There was lots of cuddling and kissing. So of course he became very attached to me, whether in front of the camera or off. It wasn't long before he was asking to come home with me, and I'd agree, thinking he would be the perfect playmate for Suzanne. How foolish was that? It was enough that children in school who had seen *Julia* were already innocently asking her about her brother.

"I don't have a brother," she'd have to tell them.

When Suzanne was ten or so, she became very quiet and withdrew into herself. One night when she was invited to sleep over with friends, I could hear her begging not to be sent home to me. I knew she was justified. She probably felt more loved and tended to by the mother of her friend than she did around me. But if I acknowledged what I was hearing from my daughter, it would have meant I'd have to change my life dramatically and I could not deal with that. I'd seen my mother leaving her husband and younger child behind in order to follow me, and I knew it was negligent. Yet I also knew it was different for me because it was essential that I travel for work. Work made me rich both financially and emotionally.

I chose to leave Suzanne home the summer of 1972, when David Frost and I were invited to join Aristotle and Jackie Onassis in Greece. Suzanne had been invited. Other children were going to be there with their nannies and they were all Suzanne's age. But I was wary. I had no idea how children were treated in a family such as the Onassises, and I did not know what the daily routine was on that island and yacht. Perhaps I was wrong, but I simply did not trust that it would work for my twelve-year-old daughter.

We flew over on Ari's airline, *Olympic,* and the service was superb. Jackie met us when we arrived by boat on the island of

Skorpios. She looked adorable in a short little skirt, scarf, and big sunglasses resting on her head. She was wearing no makeup or jewelry, and it told me her defenses were down for a casual and intimate visit.

I, of course, arrived with full makeup and a mountain of luggage. Why not? My host was a man who'd been a longtime lover of Maria Callas. My hostess was a style icon who brought culture, taste, and Oleg Cassini to the White House. I was not going to show up without a full wardrobe. Even when I'm dressing casual, each detail is always excruciatingly considered.

The Onassis compound was stunning. It sat on a verdant hillside looking out over the crystalline Aegean Sea, which is dotted with rocky islands. One of the rooms in the mansion was reserved for Winston Churchill's use. I asked a butler to open it for me one day and remember seeing impressive photographs and his cigars. The terrace where we dined had the feel of a magnificent magical cave, lit with candles and with comfortable big sofas all around. It overlooked the sea, of course, which you could see rippling below until the last light of sunset. Then the stars came out, shining as bright as any I'd ever seen.

We dined in caftans and little silver slippers—all vaguely Middle Eastern, as I recall—or whatever the look would have been in 1970 of jet-set Greek-island chic. Lee Radziwell, Jacqueline Onassis' younger sister, was there. But I don't remember any conversations. I was exhausted from the flight, which followed an engagement I had had that required my doing two shows a night. I do remember observing the children, sun-kissed and gorgeous, and I kept thinking about whether their routine would have suited Suzanne. They were with staff most of the day, except when there was an outing, sail, or game of tennis. Then, before dinner, the children were brought in to join the adults having cocktails. They were already fed, and after spending about an hour with the adults, playing games and making conversation, they were whisked away to bed by staff, while their mothers did not move.

There was simply no room for the children to have their own preferences. And I thought to myself that it would not have worked for Suzanne, who was used to asserting herself when we were together.

Even I was having a difficult time asserting my own preferences. I remember it caused David some discomfort when I asked after one evening that I be left alone in the morning to sleep in. I woke up on the yacht and everyone had gone off in a launch boat. I went up to the top deck, where my breakfast was waiting, and I sat under a big, beautiful umbrella in a big, beautiful sun hat. The boat was rocking only the slightest bit and the most perfect breeze was cooling the air. I looked out at all the islands rising out of the sea and it was just magnificent. I was at the peak of my career and in love with a fabulous man who seemed to constantly take me to wonderful places to meet wonderful people. I remember thinking, "This is fantastic. This view, this breakfast, this yacht, these people who are so charming, and this gentleman who cares for me so deeply. I have such a wonderful life." I felt as if I had climbed to the top of the world that morning. Yet something was missing. I wasn't sure I was really in love with David. But the other part of it was that I had gone away on a vacation to this enchanted place without my daughter.

My reasons for doing so might have been appropriate. But I still felt guilty.

I missed her. And I imagined that despite our issues, she was missing me.

You'd think that with all my distractions from mothering, I'd be less controlling than your average mom. That was not the case. When Suzanne was ready for high school, again, as my way of giving her the best education she could possibly have, I put her in boarding school, first in Northern California, then in Switzerland. It was what people of means did with their children. She always invited me to visit her in these schools, and I was pleased to know she wanted me around. When she graduated, I took her to Paris for a shopping spree. She agreed to the trip. But shopping was my way to celebrate, not hers. It just shows you how little I was in touch with my own daughter's priorities.

When she didn't apply to Harvard, I was beyond disappointed and far too dramatic in letting her know it. One of the great dreams of her mother and her grandparents was now being deferred, not quite like a "raisin in the sun," but perhaps a very expensive sun-dried tomato. My whole life I'd regretted not getting my college degree. My parents did as well. Even a degree from New York University instead of their dream school, Howard University, would have satisfied their hunger for the status of having a daughter with a college degree.

"Why didn't you apply to Harvard?" I asked Suzanne one summer day at home.

"It's too big and too conservative," she said, making points that any other parent would have accepted and understood. "I really want to go to Wesleyan."

"Wesleyan," I gasped. "Where is it?"

We would soon find out. Because that fall, we found our-selves in one of the classic adolescent rites of passage, the East Coast college tour. Only ours wasn't quite as classic as Su-zanne had wanted it to be. You see, her oh-so-fabulous mother could not leave well enough alone. Instead of taking campus tours like normal civilians, I had contacted each college in advance to let them know we were coming. I was insensitive enough as a mother to think that was the best way to go about things. So we'd arrive (without police escort, but with my sense of importance lending an air of grandiosity to the pro-ceedings) and be greeted by a college president or special en-voy. And I'd be in a fur coat, with my hair done just so, and in my finest fall ensembles, marching around shaking hands like something between a presidential candidate and the director of a cotillion.

"Hello there," I'd say. "How do you do!" Suzanne had ev-ery right to be thinking, "I wish this woman would just leave me alone." But she never said a word.

When we were asked to special VIP luncheons at the fac-ulty club with all the muckety-mucks, frequently including the college president, questions would be addressed to me, not her. I wasn't even aware enough to see how much this hurt her. It was my "Diahann Carroll Road Show," not hers, and when I'd detect even an ounce of discontent, I'd be shocked. I'd say to her, "Maybe it's a challenge having a mother in show business, but if I had not been in show business, then I would never have met your father, who has been so wonderful to you and has been able to offer you so much!"

She'd say, "You don't understand." And then we'd drive to another college.

Wesleyan, it turned out, was a prestigious small school in Connecticut, known for its liberal and creative student body and excellent courses in the humanities. If Suzanne had to face issues there that had to do with being my daughter, I never witnessed them. She did tell me that when she was moving in freshman year, some girls came into her dorm room and told her that Diahann Carroll's daughter was in the class.

"Oh yeah?" Suzanne replied coolly.

"Her last name isn't Carroll, but we think it's the name on that pile of Louis Vuitton luggage over there," one of them said about some suitcases that did not belong to Suzanne. "Uh-huh," is all she said in response.

Later, someone saw a family photo in Suzanne's room and figured out who she was.

"Is that your mother?" she was asked.

"Yes," she replied. "And now I know who my friends will be around here."

She handled that episode well, but I was sorry it had to happen. She wanted to be seen for who she was, not as the child of someone people knew from television. Not that every child of a celebrity finds the privilege associated with a famous parent a burden. Some are more than happy to use their connections. But Suzanne, always a top student with her own taste and strong ideas, preferred to find her own identity. And she did so impressively. After Wesleyan, she was accepted at the Columbia School of Journalism, a rigorous and highly selective program. She did well there and went about getting jobs after graduate school, one as an intern for the *MacNeil-Lehrer News Hour* on PBS and then at CNN in Atlanta, where she wrote the news. She was an editor at *Essence* and an anchor, along with Greg Kinnear, in the early days of *E!*

Without any string pulling from me or her father, Suzanne had become an in-demand young talent in Los Angeles. The agents for Connie Chung and Diane Sawyer flew to Los Angeles to meet with her to suggest she sign with them and move to New York for the grooming that takes an anchor from one step to the next. She turned them down. She didn't want to devote herself to a career that would take over her life and make her spend hours a day in wardrobe and makeup. *Lost* is not a strong enough word to explain my disappointment. I knew she "had it," as they say. She was beautiful on camera, charming beyond belief, and funny as hell. Still, she walked with no regrets, and never looked back. I should have applauded such a decision. But I was too stuck on the idea that fame and fortune were all that mattered. My daughter was emotionally mature and confident enough to know that the good life being offered to her was not in a world she craved. I could not see it. So I created yet another mother-daughter impasse. But let me be clear—we always loved each other.

Well, I was never anything like a "Mommie Dearest."

I had, however, become Norma Desmond in Toronto. And in 1997, Suzanne flew up to see me with a very specific purpose. She wanted me to meet her intended. I have to laugh when I think of his first glimpse of me onstage, playing a conniving, demented, facial-obsessed diva preying on a younger man. He was lovely, but I had never met him before. The problem was Suzanne just sprang the news of their marriage plans on me at dinner without warning. My shock was apparent. Why couldn't she have waited a while? If I knew then what I know now—from the golden throne of my golden years—I would have calmly listened to her and approved. Young people interested in getting married aren't really open to anyone else's opinions, just blessings and congratulations. What did I do instead? I ran into the ladies' room and broke into tears. Why couldn't I just get over myself and show my daughter I supported her?

Not long after that, a letter came to me in Toronto. It was beautiful and poignant, not angry or spiteful, explaining she was now married. I didn't take it like a mature sixty-two-year-old woman. Why should I? In the kind of melodramatic style one associates with starlets with entitlement issues, I fell to my dressing-room floor and started crawling around on my hands and knees. Eventually my assistant suggested I stop making a scene. I had just had my nightly meltdown onstage, and that was enough strain on my vocal cords for one evening.

The thing is, Suzanne knew exactly what she was doing. She had figured out how to have a simple wedding that removed the need for family and family drama, keeping me and my scene-stealing ways and wardrobe out of it. When I look back on it now, I was a fool for not trusting Suzanne's instincts for building a great new life.

It was wonderful to watch her hold my little grandson for the first time. She took to mothering with such devotion. Suddenly she had a chance to do everything right that I did wrong, and I was overjoyed to see her sense of purpose and focus. And it changed the way I saw her, too. In fact, the healing effect it had on our relationship was huge. Someone had finally come along who was going to be a bigger star in the family than I was: this sweet little baby.

But, oh, did it hurt when she moved her family overseas in 2003, and then had her second child, a daughter. I went to visit several times, and as impressive as her surroundings were, more impressive was how delightful it was to walk around with her family through markets and gardens and along the beaches, and not have anyone interfere in our private moments.

Once again, Suzanne knew what she wanted. She had been so inspired by their surroundings that she and her husband wrote and directed their first film about the culture. It had its American premiere at the Tribeca Film Festival, and the event brought Sidney Poitier, his two daughters, and me together. It was a wonderful night to be in Suzanne's shadow as I watched her with Sidney's two daughters, all of them so composed, articulate, and beautiful. They were three successful, self-assured, and statuesque women, doing what they wanted to do with their lives. And despite their tumultuous upbringings, with show-business parents who didn't know what to do with themselves or their overwrought love affair, they had grown up and come through beautifully. Everything had worked out for them just fine.

"We must have done something right," I told Sidney later.

Now Suzanne and her family live in Europe. Of course I long for them to live closer. But if I know anything now, it's that when things can't be perfect, good can be plenty good enough. Suzanne knows I enjoy our holidays together immensely. And having grandchildren has given me a whole new lease on life. One of the first things I learned from these two little ones is that it's important for people to actually be able to touch and hug you. So I now own play clothes that are expressly for my visits with them. They're made of these wonderful fabrics that you can just throw into the washing machine. Isn't that remarkable? When they get dirty, they don't have to go to the dry cleaners! Imagine!

To play with children properly, you have to be able to get right down on the floor with them. And that's what I do. We play with trains and dollhouses and Suzanne cannot believe what she is seeing. I observe the look on her face when she sees Diahann Carroll letting two little children climb all over her. She must be thinking, "Who is this woman playing on the floor with my children?" She is a stunning mother who understands full well how important it is to give yourself over to your children. Yet she manages to find time to work on her film projects. The other day I had to laugh because when I called her, she was much too busy writing a screenplay to talk to me. I hung up the phone and remembered all the years I hardly had a moment for her because of work, and I thought, "My how the tables have turned! Good for her!"

These days, I am more preoccupied with the lives of my grandchildren than with my own. It's shocking to me, but there it is. One of the nicest moments as a grandmother came not long ago, when Suzanne let her children have their first sleepover in my home. Bath time is absolute heaven with those two. My grandson can be very commanding. "I need some toys in here, Nana," he has told me. "But no ducks please. I really don't want any ducks!" There is nothing better than the rhythmic sound of two little ones breathing softly as they sleep in your bed.

Last Christmas I went to visit them in Europe with my suitcases so full of presents I couldn't get them up the stairs. Immediately after dinner, my granddaughter excused herself from the table and reappeared moments later in a completely different outfit. She said, "Nana, Mommy told me you sent this for me." Then a few minutes later, she went and changed into something else I'd brought her. She must have changed outfits five times. I had been shopping for her all year, sending clothes from New York and Los Angeles, and although Suzanne had originally requested nothing that had to be dry-cleaned, it wasn't long before I was realizing that wash-and-wear clothes, even for children, just don't have the look I love. I love those little pleated kilts and wool overcoats of the John John and Caroline school of dressing. I like starched-collar dresses on girls and blazers on little boys. Darling, and totally impractical! As my granddaughter kept changing into one high-maintenance ensemble after the next (my favorite was a navy-blue taffeta number suitable for a debutante ball) Suzanne and I exchanged loving looks. Then we laughed at each other. Nothing had to be said. In her adult years, she has come to accept that Diahann Carroll is Diahann Carroll. None of these clothes were going into the washing machine. And if her little girl was becoming a clotheshorse under my tutelage, why fight the force of human nature?

"God is punishing you, Suzanne," I said. "This time with the reincarnation of me. It won't be long before she's wearing couture."

We played with games, made drawings, and measured one another's height, back-to-back. "Look how big you are," I told my grandson. "Yes," he said with all seriousness. "I'm a very big boy." When we were going over to see some of their friends for lunch one day and it started to drizzle, I didn't balk when Suzanne suggested we hop onto a crowded old bus. The last time I was on a bus, I can't even remember. High school, maybe? I sat down next to a woman who clearly was not in her right mind. She was holding a little dog to her chest that had fur quite similar to that of my sable coat. Suzanne looked anxious that I would be put off and annoyed. But I just patted the dog's head and said, "Nice doggy," and left it at that. Later, Suzanne wrote to friends and family that on a bus, in the rain, and wherever we went that holiday week, "Mom was a trouper." I have spent my life charming big audiences of strangers. This was the best review I could ever hope to receive.

I did not stay at Suzanne and her husband's house. Even a trouper can only take so much activity when she's jet-lagged. Besides, the children loved visiting me at my nearby hotel. One day they came to pick me up, all looking absolutely divine. My granddaughter was in a kilt with a little black velvet jacket. My grandson was in a sports jacket and tie. We were going to the ballet.

"These children have been entirely dressed by Diahann Carroll," Suzanne said playfully.

A woman nearby was impressed by how adorable they looked.

"Are those your grandchildren?" she asked.

"Yes, and I'm in charge of wardrobe," I said.

It was a wonderful holiday. I can't remember a time since those children were born that our visits haven't been wonderful. And when it was time for me to fly home, they didn't want me to go. I hugged Suzanne good-bye, and she told me she loved me.

Are there any words a mother wants to hear more than those?

I don't think so. My mother must be very happy for us.

These days, I acknowledge the cost of my successes. Suzanne and I are finally at a place of love and laughter . . . and the place is often on the floor playing with her children.

I still remember the day I was at a playground with my granddaughter, who I think of as Miss Bossy. She wanted to go down a slide.

"Nana, come here," she said.

"Okay, darling, here I am," I said as I stood beside her.

"No, not there, Nana, up here with me!"

"It's okay, honey," I said. "I'll just stand here and help you down."

"No, Nana, you have to slide down with me!"

I didn't want to do it. The old bones are not what they once were.

But she was not taking no for an answer. So in a crowded playground, I found myself climbing up a ladder and sitting next to my tiny granddaughter, then wrapping my arm around her and pushing off.

"Whee!" we said as we slid down. She thought this was the funniest thing she had ever done. We were both laughing hysterically. And while we were doing so, a smiling woman I didn't know approached us.

"Isn't it wonderful?" she said. "She doesn't even know you're Diahann Carroll!"

"I can't even begin to tell you," I replied. "It's magnificent."

SEVEN

What Mirror, Where?

IT WAS THE NIGHT BEFORE MY PLASTIC SURGERY AND I was very nervous. I paced around my apartment, frustrated that I couldn't have a drink to calm down, and didn't even want to take a sleeping pill. I wanted to go into my surgery as healthy as I could be. I had been eating very carefully and exercising rigorously in the months before the procedure in order to have my body in its best fighting shape.

I'm used to having my face scrutinized and fussed over. But the idea of going under the knife was very frightening to me. And you hear of occasional botched procedures, and of course you can't help but worry. Can you imagine a more vacuous reason for a medical emergency? Please! Is plastic surgery really worth the risk and the immense expense? Besides, why not respect every wrinkle on your face? Isn't that the most positive way to greet the aging process, rather than taking desperate measures to reverse it? Yes, I paid for my wrinkles by living through everything I have lived through in my life. But that doesn't mean I want to look at them in the mirror.

I know this sounds like rampant vanity and artificiality. Well, what can I say?

I'm a performer who still really enjoys make-believe. I remember being in a dressing room on the set of *Grey's Anatomy* a couple years ago with the little daughter of one of the actresses. She must have been four or five years old, and she was fascinated by my false eyelashes. Clearly they were not something her mother appreciated. But I couldn't help myself. "Would you like to try them on?" I asked the little girl.

She did, and was smitten. Her mother didn't look convinced.

But why not give them a try? I'm for whatever makes you happy.

High heels, makeup, sable coats, and beautiful jewelry. That's my platform.

The other day a woman came up to me at a party and told me she still remembered my entrance in *No Strings*. I told her how wonderful it was to hear that.

"You were carrying the most beautiful handbag I'd ever seen," she said, gushing.

She didn't remember my entrance. But she will never forget my handbag.

And Harry Belafonte will never forget coming over on one of my at-home maintenance days in the early 1960s. I had warned him in advance that I would not be a pretty sight, but he really needed to speak to me about a recording he was working on. I had refused to run out of the house at a moment's notice for the meeting.

"I can't jump in the shower and be ready in twenty minutes, Harry," I told him. "I'm just not one of those people."

So he came over, and when I opened my door, he nearly had a heart attack. I had avocado in my hair and maybe mayonnaise as well, and egg white all over my face. Delicious. And I was also wearing a rubber suit to take the excess water out of my body. On my feet were clown-size terry-cloth slippers to absorb all the perspiration. So one of the most beautiful men in the world, a man whom every woman desired, with his beautiful face and broad shoulders and slim hips, was looking at me in this awful state, and if there had been any misguided feelings of attraction between us, they were instantly gone.

"Oh my God," he said as he stumbled back at the sight of me. "I can't believe you actually let me come by here to see you like this. You have no interest in me at all!"

That was the last time I allowed anyone to see me at home in this condition. In fact, for years, when I was doing my big shows on the road, I would not allow room service to deliver my breakfast. It had to be brought in by someone I employed, someone I trusted.

Makeup? Don't bother telling me you want to see me without it. The last time friends did that, I listened to them, and appeared without anything on my face. They asked, "Are you okay, Diahann? You don't look well." Like I've said before, I don't know who I am until I put on my makeup. But give me a little time and I'm good to go!

I once read somewhere—some philosopher said this—that human identity is nothing but a series of masks. You take one away and there's another mask below it. I totally relate to that idea. At the core of me is a woman who revels in artifice.

Artifice isn't just fun: it's my "architecture." So when friends tell me they want to see me with my makeup off, I figure they really don't know me that well. I mean, I was raised by a mother who put me in Shirley Temple curls! Why should I accept what I'm given when I can have it made to look like anything I want?

So if there's a medical procedure to take some wrinkles away and bring everything up, sign me on! Some people just don't have fun unless they're looking their best. And I'm one of them. To me, owning who you are means asking yourself "What do I have to do today to make myself happy?" Yet there's still such shame around plastic surgery. I know people who finish one procedure and say, "Phew! That's over!" But I know that in a year they'll go back for more, and won't admit it. We know who we are. We're the ones wearing big sunglasses in restaurants.

I guess I'm lucky it took until my late sixties for me to break down and agree that it was time to address the situation. It started when I was aghast seeing a picture of myself on the cover of a magazine. My press agent told me I was crazy.

"You look wonderful," he told me.

"If you can't see I need plastic surgery, you're fired," I replied.

I consulted with a famous surgeon in New York, who is so private that he has a special side door for patients who don't want to run into anyone else in the waiting area. I told him my face needed a little help, that things were falling down and we had to get them up again. He showed me some photos and then we decided it would be better for me to get the work done in Los

Angeles, where I'd be close to home. So I went to visit a surgeon not far from where I live who came highly recommended. He felt good about my prospects and fine with my preference for a gentle job. I didn't feel I wanted him to do anything at all near my eyes; it just worried me too much and I didn't want that pulled-up look. He persuaded me to trust him and said that I'd be very satisfied with the results.

"And because you're doing this now," he said, "you should be able to wait years before doing anything again. You're the perfect patient."

This surgeon was very serious and had a stellar reputation. The people I knew who had had work done by him told me that the only thing I was going to dislike was that I'd end up wishing I'd been pulled a little tighter. But I didn't want that. I don't need to look as smooth as a plum. I don't need automaton eyes that are in a permanent look of surprise. I can live with a wrinkle or two. Human works for me.

So I went in for the procedure and don't remember a thing except that when I woke up, I was not in any pain, and I stayed right there in a room near the office for a few days, healing in a spalike environment, a very nice option I was offered. When the bandages came off after a few days, I was still puffy. But then, a week later, I began to look more like myself. And I thought, "Isn't this nice? I don't look like I've been yanked like a mannequin. I just look like a better and more rested version of myself." People noticed when I started going out and about. They'd tell me, "You look wonderful."

Not long after that, I was the oldest guest on an *Oprah Winfrey Show* about "Aging Brilliantly." Nora Ephron was on the show, too. Her baleful, funny book about aging as a woman, *I Feel Bad About My Neck,* was hitting the bestseller list that season. She was forthright and funny about the havoc that aging has wreaked on her self-image. "Do you know what you get as a present for your sixty-second birthday?" she asked. "A mustache! . . . Which is why we have waxing, darling!" At some point, Oprah looked at me and asked, "Is this what seventy-one looks like?" I told her it was. And the audience broke into spontaneous and thunderous applause.

I should have added, "But it's with a little help from my plastic surgeon" right away. But later in the show, I did find myself yelling, "I believe in plastic surgery! I want the world to know! Oh God, yes! Absolutely, I would not be without it!"

Okay, maybe I was a little too zealous. But I've seen how getting older torments my friends and colleagues. And in my business, there's only one response to an actress who turns forty. *Don't!* The aging process is always harder for women than for men. I've heard people say that getting older is beautiful. I think it is, but inside, not out. Women are not happy about aging. I look into the eyes of some of my friends and I see worry and sadness because they don't know whether to give up or fight. It's hard to live in a society so hung up on age. Even for the most beautiful women, things fall apart. I sympathize and I commiserate. But I also like making suggestions that will help.

I let it slip that I've had plastic surgery if I know it'll open the door for a woman who would be happier with it than without it. I push acupuncture and all kinds of facials and spa treatments, too. And there's nothing I love more than taking someone in need along for a little maintenance outing. I have gone with friends for all kinds of treatments with such peculiar-sounding names that I don't always understand what they are. The other day I took a neighbor I adore to get our faces ironed.

Hey, if I can do it for my hair, why not my face?

Hair. It isn't only on our heads. It's on our minds, constantly.

I'm sure there are people who think the nicest hair is the most natural hair. I'm not one of them. I have been a friend of the press-and-curl ever since my Shirley Temple–curl days. And blond is in these days, no matter what your ethnicity. There's one hair salon in Beverly Hills where black women come out with hair as straight and blond as Donatella Versace's. What really amazes me is that there are plenty of men out there who believe it's natural, bless them. A couple years ago, I was fortunate enough to be invited to a luncheon for an influential, successful group of black women in Hollywood. We were twenty-five of the most successful black women in show business, young and old, many of us young stars, and it was just so inspiring to be part of the group, all of us doing so well. The outfits were wonderful, and all were clearly as carefully considered as they'd be for a red-carpet event. When you are in show business, you can never forget that you are a product, and you must always be aware of your packaging. Anyway, I have to say, superficial as it sounds, I was fascinated by the hair I was seeing at this luncheon. So many of these young stars were wearing long blond hair and obviously enjoying tossing it around with the insouciance of cheerleaders. There was not the least bit of self-consciousness in the room. Happily, I felt right at home among them. In fact, I do believe I was one of the forerunners of black women lightening their hair. I learned from my stylist that lightening your hair—as long as it's complimentary to your skin tone—can take years off your appearance.

It's no news flash. Hair is a big deal, especially for blacks. And I've done it all, from hair to eternity. As a professional performer, nobody knows better that I do that time is money and so is hair. In fact, my hair once cost the movie *Hurry Sundown* a very handsome sum.

It was 1966, and the great Otto Preminger was once again my director.

When I heard the filming would be in humid New Orleans, and that much of it would be shot on location, I knew the weather would be troublesome for everyone, particularly the black actors, when it came to hair. So I made an appointment with Mr. Preminger in his New York office. It was on Fifth Avenue, right across the street from the Plaza, where I was living with my daughter while doing my show there.

His office was huge and imposing, modern, high up, and hushed, looking down over midtown Manhattan. Preminger was a small Austrian man, elegant but not formal.

"Mr. Preminger, thank you for taking the time to see me," I said across his desk.

"Yes, of course, but what is it?" he asked.

"Well, I was wondering who you've hired to do hair for the film."

"I've hired my wife's hairdresser, who has the best salon in New York."

My heart sank. Any other young actress would have stopped right there. I don't even know what gave me the nerve to request this meeting in the first place. This was a very important director. But since I've never been one to hold my tongue, I went on.

"I understand the weather can be very humid in New Orleans."

"Yes? So?" He was tapping a pen on his desk, and I was getting more nervous.

"Well, humidity can have a strong effect on hair. So I'd just like to make this suggestion because I'm not sure you've ever had to deal with this before."

"What is the suggestion, Miss Carroll?"

"Well, it would be wonderful if someone was on the set who could straighten out frizzy hair. Does this man who does your wife's hair know anything about straightening hair? Because he might need to have some understanding of curling irons, pressing combs, and hair relaxants."

With that, the great director, whose temper had earned him the nickname "Otto the Terrible," jumped out of his seat. He was shorter than I was, and it seemed to me that sparks were shooting out of his eyes. I could see at that moment why he'd been cast as a Nazi officer in a Broadway play and two films. I leaned back from his anger.

"Are you telling me who to hire for this film?" he said. "I never allow any actor to dictate how I should direct a film. I wouldn't allow Elizabeth Taylor to tell me how to do her hair in a film, and I won't allow it from you!"

Outside his office, phones had been ringing nonstop. He was a very busy man with too much on his plate.

"Whatever you say, sir," I said as I stood with bowed head. "Whatever you say."

I had to laugh as I left his office. He and I had been in a hair situation years before, over my bandanna in *Porgy and Bess*. I suspected, though, fond as I was of him, that he was going to eat his words on the set of *Hurry Sundown*.

Being the conscientious, or perhaps *controlling* performer that I am, I called his wife's hairdresser, introduced myself as a supporting actress on the picture, and invited him to see my show at the Plaza. Afterward, he came to say hello in my dressing room, and I introduced him to my hairstylist, who tried to show him what he did with my hair. But this man took one look at the equipment, which was really pretty basic (hot comb, curling iron, and assorted hair products), and he said, "I really don't know anything about any of this," and left without further discussion.

One evening, months later, we were on the *Hurry Sundown* set in New Orleans. We were shooting the star-studded film about racism, greed, and emotional unrest in the contemporary South on a front porch, and lo and behold, it started to drizzle. I was doing a scene with Robert Hooks, a wonderful leading man. There were several pieces of equipment on the set. There was, in particular, this very large crane that Mr. Preminger was inside of, high above us, which was costing him a fortune to rent for the evening. As we rehearsed the scene, he came floating down with the camera, all very slowly, to almost close-up distance.

While Mr. Preminger was behind the camera Robert whispered to me, "You're getting wet."

I knew my hair was frizzing up. I could feel it happening; your hair just gets bigger and asserts itself when it's raining. I was wearing a hairpiece, but some of my real hair was showing, and it was changing from moment to moment. And so this little god in the sky, Otto Preminger, in his big yellow crane, started yelling, "Hairdresser!" And this poor New York hairdresser named Leonard came out and started to fuss with my hair. Otto was bright red, beet red, up in his bright yellow crane.

"What should I do?" this hairdresser asked me in a panic. "The hair has to match the previous shot. You know that!"

"I don't know," I told him. "But when we met in my dressing room at the Plaza, I tried to show you things you'd need to protect yourself in a situation like this."

He desperately tried to repair my hair, then he ran. "I don't know what else to do," he said.

So we started shooting again, and the crane was coming down again slowly, and Robert and I were doing our serious scene from this serious melodrama about race and the Deep South, and Mr. Preminger was seeing that my hair was getting larger and larger, in the weather, and sticking out in very unsightly ways, and he became furious.

"Cut," he yelled. "This isn't going to match. This isn't going to match!"

I couldn't take it all very seriously. Because while we were shooting, the cast was experiencing racism firsthand in Louisiana that was very anxiety-producing. One evening my party had been asked to leave a restaurant because I was black. We never knew whether or not we'd be turned away when we black actors went out with our fellow cast members Jane Fonda, Michael Caine, Faye Dunaway. I decided to speak to one of the associate producers of the film and find out if he could call restaurants in advance to prepare them so there would not be any scenes. He made sure we were accompanied by bodyguards to prevent harassment.

Eventually, Mr. Preminger calmed down. Then he asked me what to do. He trusted me because he knew how serious I was about my work.

"So are you really asking me what to do?" I asked.

He said, "Yes, I am."

"Is there another scene you can shoot instead of mine?"

He said no.

"You have to call the day, then," I said.

And he did. He sent everybody home. And when we were walking back to his car, I said, "I can't tell you how sorry I am that this happened to your production." He asked me again what I would recommend. I told him it would be difficult getting a black hairdresser into the union quickly who understood what to do with our hair. But I did mention someone from New York, and then an associate producer actually found someone who lived closer. This man turned out to be brilliant at pressing, curling, and styling, and Mr. Preminger thanked me, and everything was fine on the hair front from then on. The movie was another story. I didn't care for it because it really didn't advance anything politically. It just showed poor blacks being kicked around by racist whites. But you know what? One more black man got into the union because of that film, so in a way it did have a positive political effect.

A few years later, on *Julia*, I helped integrate the hair and makeup department at Fox. Again, it wasn't political. It was practical. I simply didn't have time to drive to the hair salon that knew how to deal with my hair at the level necessary for television. And I was too busy learning lines to do my hair at home, which is what other black actresses did. But Fox had never had a black woman starring in a show. The makeup person they had wasn't accustomed to dealing with a black leading lady, either. She thought she knew how to do my makeup because she'd done Lena Horne's. I asked if that meant that she used the same makeup for all white actresses. (We all have different skin tones that grab the camera in different ways, and all that has to be dealt with carefully in a medium as unforgiving as television.) It didn't take long for the studio to realize it had to bring in experts for all types of black hair, and makeup artists, to deal with the likes of me.

And they did.

Eventually, I realized life would be simpler with wigs. I can still remember my conversion. I was performing a couple shows a night at the Americana Hotel in New York. My stylist arrived to wash my hair between shows. One evening we were both stunned as we watched my hair floating down the drain. It was absolutely frightening, but my hair had been pressed and curled and processed to the point of collapse. My stylist told me, "Wait there, I'll be right back!" And he returned with a bag full of wigs. I tried them on, and thought, "Not bad, and we can improve on it tomorrow." I was just amazed at how much easier wigs made my life. I believe in them enough to put my name on a line of them. But I'll be honest, as I became more discriminating, I started to prefer very expensive ones. Hand-tied wigs are easiest to work with and are my personal favorites.

Looking like a million bucks everywhere you go isn't cheap.

I learned that at an early age. It wasn't just the influence of my mother, who once made me swear I wouldn't tell my father she'd spent a hundred dollars on a pair of shoes. I learned about paying for quality from my dear departed friend Josephine Premice, a naturally elegant woman who had exquisite taste in everything in life. She once eyed my new blue cloth coat with a detachable fur collar. I was thrilled with it.

"Darling, we either wear fur or we wear cloth," she told me. "That combination isn't working." It was a lesson I took with me the rest of my life.

When it came time to dress for my nightclub bookings, I steered clear of jewelry and chose couture gowns with simple lines to create the look of a proper chanteuse. It wasn't long before I was wearing designs by Jimmy Galanos, Bill Blass, Arnold Scaasi, and Norman Norrell. Later, Bob Mackie, a creative titan, designed for me, too, and continues to do so to this day!

The first time Norman Norrell along with Ray Agayan invited me to the debut of one of his collections, in the late 1950s, I was an absolute novelty in the room. The women invited to these shows were buyers, editors, and wealthy New York socialites.

What was a young black singer and actress doing among them?

Designers loved me and they wanted me there. I had the slim, long body they loved for their clothes and they liked the way I moved in them. When it came time for me to play a fashion model in Paris, for *No Strings,* I wanted Arnold Scaasi to do the costumes, and he wanted to do them, too. We had a meeting in 1961, and were all set to go. Arnold loves show business and is a real theater buff, and he was very excited. But his associate would not allow it. She believed that he would alienate all his buyers in the South if he did something so high profile for a black woman. Years later, when I heard this story for the first time, I couldn't hold it against him. You see, Arnold and I understand that business is business. Besides, if I'd taken offense, I never would have had the chance to meet John F. Kennedy while wearing his wonderful, white, tight, double-breasted suit with brass buttons. Arnold recalls the president looking dazzled. And from what I recall, the taupe satin ball gown with navy blue bodice that Arnold put me in when I sang a song from *Yentl* (at the request of Barbra Streisand) for the 1984 Golden Globes dazzled Aaron Spelling enough to put me on *Dynasty*.

I guess I was enough of a style icon when I was younger that JCPenney wanted to put my name on my own clothing line in the early 1990s. Why not? We did upscale looks—suits, blazers, skirts with a little kick—at rock-bottom prices. It was fun, but not easy logistically, and I learned quickly that I'd rather wear clothes than make them.

I loved being on the International Best Dressed list and I still love fashion, though I sometimes have to remind people who I am. Not long ago, I called Oscar de la Renta, who had done some lovely dresses for me in the past. I said, "Hello, Mr. de la Renta, it's Diahann Carroll." He said, 'Who?'" It's not the same as it was when any top designer would see me at a moment's notice.

And I have to admit, I can't wear the small sizes I used to wear. Some shops in Beverly Hills are so proud of having all these dresses in size zero. I don't think that size even existed when I was young. I was a size five, and everyone considered that small. So when I find a garment I like on Rodeo Drive, I ask shop clerks, who are always tiny, "Do you know if the designer makes this dress in a size for a real person?"

"What do you mean?" they ask.

"Well, I really love this coat, but I need it in a size twelve," I reply.

There's usually an awkward silence. Then they tell me the coat doesn't come in such a big size. So I lean in and quietly tell them to do me a favor and get on the phone and ask. And they scurry off, then come back to me with stunned looks on their faces.

"Ms. Carroll! Guess what? They do make the coat in size twelve!"

"No shit," I say.

And then we laugh.

Now, I'm not saying I plan to get any bigger. God forbid. But I'm not uncomfortable being a size that's normal for women of my age. And there's always the siren call of liposuction. But for now, I'm going to keep up the maintenance by exercising. I love to walk around my neighborhood, which has lots of hills. I enjoy walking to dinner nearby, too. I walk past trees in bloom and gated mansions, and right past the spot where Barbara Sinatra was mugged across the street from my apartment building. If anyone ever tried to mug me, I'd be in shape to either run or deck them. In my building, I have a health spa and gym, which I use daily unless I'm on the road. I've taken the discipline of my art and applied it to the body and I get help from my expert personal trainer, Romy, who gently puts me through my paces. I run on the treadmill, lift weights, and do yoga and Pilates. Romy says I'm one of her best clients, and I have the stamina of many who are far younger than me. So who cares if I'm a size twelve?

Regular exercise is a must, because no matter your genes, the body starts to break down. Without stimulation and attention, the muscles will deteriorate quickly. I eat well, too, which, of course, can be a bit of a bore at times. And, of course, I've been "on holiday"—at the plastic surgeon's! No, I'm not perfect. I like the occasional bowl of pasta. I guess I should be pushing myself harder to follow through on any number of health resolutions each year.

But you know what? I'm happy enough with myself these days, and that's wonderful.

I've got a good head on my shoulders, and a good wig, too.

Grey's Anatomy *creator/executive producer, Shonda Rhimes, and me. (Lester Cohen/WireImage for PMK/HBH)*

EIGHT

Grey Matters

HAIR AND MAKEUP WERE VERY MUCH ON MY MIND when I walked onto the set of *Grey's Anatomy* for the first time a couple of years ago. I was aware that these days, even on network television, actors share hair and makeup artists, which made me a bit uncomfortable. Growing up in film and legit theater, you were assigned your own hair and makeup artist. So when I found out that there would just be a few hair and makeup people for a dozen actors, I immediately called my team, Bruce Hutchinson, makeup, and Arthur John for hair (my team for over thirty years)—which freed me up to concentrate on my work. And when it came time for my first day of shooting, at 5 A.M., I brought Bruce in, a man highly respected in the field.

"Oh, my God, Bruce, why are you here?" people were asking him.

"I've been doing this lady's makeup for thirty years," he said.

I did not make a fuss about it. I was not a diva about it. I simply knew what I needed, and everybody was happy. When you get to be my age, it's nice to feel secure enough to know what you need and see that you have it, that's all. But you never want to assume that you're entitled to anything because of your age. That gets you nowhere. It was such a thrill to be invited to be on that show, a total delight and surprise. I had been reading about the young creator of *Grey's Anatomy*, Shonda Rhimes, a young African-American woman who came to Hollywood from Detroit and, after working extremely hard, was doing well in television as a producer and writer. I'd been told she would call, and she did.

"God, you're really tearing up the town and it's fantastic," I told her.

"Yes, and we want to know if you would honor us by becoming part of *Grey's Anatomy*," she said. She didn't ask me to audition. It was so wonderful. When I was in the prime of my career, nobody asked me to audition. But by the time I was in my late thirties, people asked me to audition all the time. I knew what they were thinking. "Let's see how she looks and make sure she isn't overweight, drinking, or on drugs. Let's see if she's stable and pretty. Maybe we can still use her." It's always nice to be asked, but it definitely lets you know where you stand when you have to go show your wares.

In the decade after the success of *Julia,* I had become known for my lavish lifestyle and volatile romances. And as much as I loved singing and made my bread and butter in nightclubs, I never had a hit album. So I had to present myself, often for jobs that felt like I was starting over again. In my early forties, things were not great; I even accepted a booking to perform at an auto show. The audience could not hear me, and then to make matters go from awful to absurd, a dog walked in off the street and lay down on the stage. Everyone in theater knows not to share the limelight with an animal—they will always upstage you. Then again, I was already being upstaged by cars. I looked at my conductor in a panic. "Keep going, just keep going," he said. So that's what I did. It's what I've done all these years.

That's why it was so lovely when Shonda Rhimes came along and asked me to play the mother of one of her leading men, a *Grey's* cardiac surgeon director named Preston Burke, played by the talented and handsome Isaiah Washington.

"Do you have anything in mind for her? Gray hair? Accent?" I asked.

"No," she said. "I have Diahann Carroll in mind."

"I'm absolutely honored," I said. "But if you want to have someone call me and tell me how you see this character, please feel free."

"No, no," she said. "I know exactly how I see her. You are her. She is you."

I hung up the phone and jumped into the air. This was a stamp of approval from an important player of the younger generation. She was saying "I buy you completely." She was saying that the dignity that people associate with my approach was something she wanted as part of her carefully hewn roster of characters. You spend your life working hard to make sure you're taken seriously. What could be more gratifying than to find out that you're still on someone's mind at an age when most actors have been discarded?

I told myself, "You really are fortunate, but don't even bother to think about how this happened. Just keep walking down this road as you've been envisioning it, because this is an industry that will take you to the moon and bury you in the mud in a week's time. Just do this job, and enjoy the ride."

And that's what I proceeded to do, without a fuss. I was to play the elegant, intelligent, and highly possessive mother of this Preston, who is engaged to marry Dr. Cristina Yang, the character played by Sandra Oh. And this is where Shonda is such a brilliant modern writer. You really didn't know if this mother I was playing was a prejudiced black woman or unable to let go of a son who seemed to need her approval for everything he did. The line she levels at the incredibly ambitious Cristina—"You don't love Preston as much as you want to be a doctor"—struck home with me, of course. After all, I'd been deeply conflicted all my life about juggling love, motherhood, and work.

Shonda knew I could relate. "I've been observing you," she told me. And I'd been observing her, too, just like I had observed in the days on movie sets with Otto Preminger. Often I found myself choked up around her, a nice young black woman running one of the most successful shows on television, a medium that has become increasingly difficult and competitive. Since my teens, I'd been dreaming of the day I would walk onto a set under complete control of an African-American who would quietly call all the shots. I saw only a moment of it when Susan Fales, the daughter of my dear friend

Josephine Premice-Fales, was a writer and producer of *A Different World*.

At the first *Grey's Anatomy* read-through, I saw Shonda sitting at the head table watching everyone, listening to everything, leaning back silently. She was taking in my work and changing the script in her head on the spot. I thought, "She's producing, directing, and writing her own series. I never thought I would see this in my lifetime." But there she was, at the head of this table. I loved it!

The work was like nothing I'd ever done before. This was a great role for me, the no-nonsense mother of a successful young man, and I was written into each show for six episodes. But it wasn't easy. I'm used to scenes being set up one shot at a time. That's how we did it in the *Dynasty* era, just like a movie. But the way a series is shot today, with the twelve main characters on the show talking at breakneck speed, was a big adjustment for me. You have to keep moving around and doing your scene even when the camera isn't on you, because while others are finishing their dialogue, the action could be shifting over to you. The very fast-moving camera lends a kind of emergency-room urgency to each scene. So you're rushing down the hall with the camera behind you until it swings off into another scene in another area. It was fascinating. And there was some very fine work being done on that set. Everybody was used to the pace. But I felt like a dinosaur in this strange new world of television, and it helped to carefully watch and learn from the other actors.

It was a privilege at my age to be a part of this.

Then, one day, things took a bad turn. There was a confrontation between Isaiah Washington, the actor playing my son, and one of his costars. One thing led to another, and Washington ultimately apologized. The apology notwithstanding, he wasn't asked to return to the show.

Now, I've seen and heard all kinds of slurs in my life. Racial, obviously. But I also heard a friend of Vic Damone's ask me why in the world I had wanted to be married to Jewish men. Once, I even heard Richard Rodgers use the word *fag* about Lorenz Hart, his collaborator before Oscar Hammerstein. We were meeting about *No Strings*, the first show he'd written without a lyricist. I can only say I felt his nervousness.

"You can't imagine how wonderful it feels," he told me, "to have written this score and not have to search all over the globe for that drunken little fag." I was stunned. This was a man whom I thought was so tasteful and tactful, and yet this remark was so unnecessarily cruel, especially in the conservative early 1960s. We were in show business, after all. Gay men were fully integrated into our world. Larry Hart may have been troubled, but his work with Rodgers included some of the most beautiful songs I ever heard, including "Where or When," "Manhattan," and "My Funny Valentine." I did not dare say a word to question the epithet. But I never really trusted Rodgers after hearing that slur, and that's why I was not shocked when, months later, he told me I wasn't invited to our Detroit opening-night party.

But if Rodgers got away with that kind of behavior, Isaiah Washington was not granted the same privilege. Nor was he given as much berth as a few other public figures who have made insensitive remarks lately. After issuing an apology, they're forgiven. It is today as it's always been, I suppose. The more seats you fill, the more the hierarchy is willing to look the other way.

I was, of course, mortified when I heard on the news that Isaiah was going to leave the cast. Or perhaps I should say what we now called "news" because this became a story that took on the importance of a national disaster. I had just completed my last episode of the season and was, of course, disappointed. I was looking forward to being part of the next season. Brian Panella, my manager, called and we assumed I would be out of the show. But a script arrived for me the next day. It was one that aired in the fall of 2007, in which I showed up to collect my son's things from his fiancée.

I loved the work and the energy on the set. But let's face it, I'm not the new belle of the ball on television—my career was not in jeopardy. The real loss was for all the fans of Isaiah.

I wish the whole incident could have been resolved the way Tiger Woods handled an unfortunate episode a few years ago. He had just won a major golf championship and was awarded a lifelong membership to a country club in the South, of which he became the first black member. Someone joked they'd have to put fried chicken on the menu for him. Tiger didn't take offense. He just laughed and said he hoped the club would continue on in the same way it always had for years, whether in the dining room, golf course, or locker room. He didn't want special treatment. But more importantly, he didn't want a fuss made about a careless remark.

A little equanimity and humor can go a long way. If you let every slur, racist or otherwise, pull you off your mark and throw you into an angry or defensive position, then you are wasting all the energy you need to move forward.

And I hope I don't offend anyone when I add that people need to give one another a little more wiggle room in general. When I heard that Don Imus was back on the air after calling a team of female college basketball players "nappy-headed hos," I wasn't as upset as others I know. It surprised even me. What he did was mean-spirited and indefensible. But for heaven's sake, he's an old man who's good at his job and has done his share of humanitarian work with children. And I enjoy him on the air. Maybe as he gets older he's having a harder time figuring out where to draw the line between irreverent and unacceptable. Yet why not give people who have apologized profusely the benefit of the doubt? And since I seem to be in my advice-giving mode here (which is not the same as finger wagging), I would say to Don and everyone else getting swept up into the heat of a moment, "Just slow down, because when you make a major mistake, it will haunt you for the rest of your life."

Everyone should just take a breath before shooting off his or her mouth, period. I hope I've learned this lesson.

Is a man really a bigot because he erupts once or twice? I would hope there's more room for forgiveness and nuance in our society. I, for one, don't think things are so black and white, if you'll excuse the pun. I'm into shades of gray, as long as they aren't in my hair.

As for me, I'm not going to worry too much about the loss of that job. It introduced me to a new audience. And best of all, it gave me the opportunity to meet Shonda Rhimes, who had invited me to participate in her prime-time show at seventy-one. She's a true force to be reckoned with in Hollywood, a quiet and gracious talent who cast several black actors in a show that has absolutely nothing to do with race.

The last time I saw Shonda I was presenting a Woman in Film Award to her. I told her I never thought I'd meet someone like her in my lifetime.

NINE

My Father, Myself

FOR THE LAST FEW YEARS OF HIS LIFE, MY FATHER and I would talk once a week on the phone. He was living in a rest home in New Jersey, near his younger sister, who is six years my senior. Even at ninety-five, John "Johnny" Johnson sounded like a kid and remained a strapping and handsome man. But he wasn't a kid anymore. His heart was weak and there would soon be cancer metastasizing in his body, and he needed help getting around. And so, after years of eating very carefully and exercising assiduously, he was finally feeling his age. I tried not to nag him too much on the phone about taking care of himself. The one thing that I did get him to do was tell his sister, Eleanor, how much he appreciated her selfless interest in him—for her invitations to dinner and offers to take him on outings on a regular basis. I am the first to confess to the self-involvement that comes with being a performer, so it always delights me to see how selfless family can be.

"Dad, tell Eleanor when you see her later how lovely she

looks," I'd remind him. He'd laugh. But he didn't argue. He knew he was charming to all women, even well into his nineties, and he knew what his compliments and attention could do for them. In the rest home, where he was one of dozens of patients, he had the nurses fussing over him as if he were their very own father. He was more dapper than any man his age.

When it became necessary for him to settle into a nursing home several years ago, it was hard to accept that it would not be near me in California. But then, we were never as close as I was with my mother. I was, after all, my mother's primary relationship in life, and I've recently come to understand that she was mine. With my father, it was more complicated. His devotion could be erratic. His demeanor could be very stern. He did not attend my first wedding in 1956 because I was marrying, as my father saw it, "the enemy," and he only came to accept my new life after Monte, my generous husband, made it clear to him that he was welcome to visit his granddaughter anytime. To his credit, Dad eventually let go of the issues he had with our interracial marriage, and we saw each other often. And oh, it was just so sweet to watch him play with Suzanne!

More than ever, I have to give him credit as a man who grew up in another time. He learned to adjust to the very different world he found himself exposed to when his daughter was getting into a career far beyond his understanding. It was not in his nature to trust white people. After all, he had seen a classmate set on fire by white men during his childhood in South

Carolina. And once, when we were driving together during my own childhood, he was stopped for no reason by a white policeman who called him "boy" and interrogated him until he was quivering with fear and rage. So for him to come to accept my first marriage was a huge step. Hell, for a man like my father, who once became furious when a well-dressed neighbor brought me into a local bar in Harlem to buy me a glass of ginger ale, and who had a hard time with a career that would bring me into contact with men and women drinking alcohol in a bar, his willingness to accept my life was a credit to his increasing open-mindedness. And what tenacity he had, to be able to escape poverty and a violent father and to build us our comfortable life!

It's impressive that he became a man of the modern world against his impulses, largely because of his love for me. But that doesn't mean he was perfect.

Many years after he came to accept my interracial marriage, primarily because of his love for his granddaughter, he pulled away from me again, when he decided to remarry. I know now it was more my fault than his. But that's because at seventy-three, at a time when I'm trying to ease up on my judgments, I see things differently. Back then, in my thirties, I was having a very hard time watching him with someone who wasn't my mother. I knew the divorce was as much her fault as his— maybe even more her fault than his, given the time she spent away from him to be with me. But that didn't mean I wasn't resentful when he brought someone new into the family. Had I been nicer to his new wife, I'm certain he would not have pulled his disappearing act.

It was the late 1970s when he first invited me to meet her. I didn't really want to, but felt I had no choice. I was living on Riverside Drive at the time, and I drove up to Westchester, where he was living in her big house. He was proud of its size and the white Cadillac she kept in the driveway. He was proud that she was a successful college graduate, too. She was younger than he was, and I think that pleased him. She also prided herself on her taste, which I, in my own small-minded way, didn't like at all. I was not in the mood for the trip to the suburbs to see them, the white carpeting in her living room that she thought was so elegant, or the ranch house he found so fabulous.

It bothered me that my father was wowed by what I saw as nothing more than a mundane lifestyle and by a deeply ambitious new wife. (Ironic, coming from me, the queen of ambition!) For my own petty reasons, I didn't like seeing him enthralled with this new woman at all. So I was quiet through our first meal. How dare this woman replace my mother? She had put a great deal of effort into dinner, and was laughing a lot. She was also bragging a little more than I cared for about the careers of people in her family and their various achievements. I really didn't want a new family. I must admit, she was doing everything she possibly could to make the evening as comfortable as it could be. My trouble was that she was just a bit too aware that I was Diahann Carroll. There were too many comments about my career and celebrity friends and not enough acknowledgment of the fact that my father had started a new life. Not that it was her place to discuss my mother. I don't know what I was expecting from our conversation, actually. But

I do know I was in no mood to discuss *Julia* or Sidney Poitier or Sammy Davis Jr. at this woman's table. Oh, was I poor company, chilly at best, and it made my father uncomfortable.

The situation worsened a few months after that, when he told me his new wife wanted me to join them at a family holiday party. I told him I didn't think it was a good idea, but they both insisted that I would enjoy the evening and told me everyone wanted to meet me. So they picked me up in the city and we drove to the house of one of her relatives in the suburbs. I sulked in the car like a morose teenager, thinking, "Why doesn't my father understand that I don't want to share my life with this new family of his?" It was very small-minded, I know, because he seemed to be so happy with this perfectly nice lady.

At the party, I found a place to sit in the corner, and was barely cordial. When it was time to leave, Dad's new wife insisted we drop by to see a relative around the corner. "He's a judge and I really want you to meet him," she said. At this point it was late in the evening, and I wanted to go home. I thought she was being inconsiderate at best, pushing this extra family visit. When we drove around the corner, the house was completely dark.

"It's right here, John," my father's new wife told my father. "Let's go!"

"But they're asleep," I argued.

"Don't worry, they'll be thrilled to meet you," she said.

I sat in the backseat, seething. But they insisted I get out of the car. She rang the doorbell several times, and I can still remember feeling mortified as the lights went on in the house. "Somebody tell me why are we doing this?" I moaned.

What I really wanted to know was how my father, who was always well mannered, could be allowing such behavior. Clearly, he was being swept up into this woman's world, and more than happy to allow her to run his life. This relative of hers and his wife came down in bathrobes, and invited us in. I was introduced as John's daughter. I found a chair in the corner and sat down. Then, as they were chatting away, this couple in their bathrobes started looking more carefully at me. Finally, one of them asked, "Aren't you Diahann Carroll?" I told them I was, apologized for waking them, and then walked to the front door. I was livid by then, and felt my father's new wife had behaved disgracefully.

She should have asked if I minded dropping by to see these people rather than forcing the situation on us. Now that I'm older and wiser, I recognize that my expectations had been way too high about how she should behave. It's really only lately, in the last ten years or so, that I have eased up a bit on what I think is and isn't correct behavior. Maybe if I'd been easier on everyone at that time, my father would not have disappeared on me, and caused me such anguish. He and his wife were moving to a new house, and when I asked for the address and phone number, he refused. "I'll get a post office box and let you know about it," he said.

He never did. I couldn't believe it. He was cutting me out of his life because of the tension between me and his wife. We stayed out of touch for several years, and it pained me constantly. To his credit, he eventually called me and I invited him to lunch at the Plaza. "I'd like that," he said. "But I can't come without my wife."

And then I said what I knew was the most important thing for him to hear.

"By all means, bring her, Dad. I'd be delighted."

We ended up having a very nice lunch. Can you believe we talked about Judith Lieber handbags, of all things? And they were also very excited to talk about a college reunion of hers they'd both attended. Neither my father nor my mother had gone to college and so a degree was always something he held in highest esteem. To have a wife with a college education and college friends delighted him, and it was one of many things this new woman brought to the relationship that he enjoyed. She was a woman of means. As I said, she was younger, and I could see how affectionate they were with each other. As I sat there with them, I saw the look of pleasure on my father's face. He was really enjoying himself and enjoying seeing that his two women were now congenial. After they left I told myself, "She is making him happy, and that's all that matters."

I had been too busy judging her to see that. He deserved happiness. So did his wife. Eventually, she became ill, and my father nursed her until her death. After that, when he'd visit me in California, it became clear that he still cared deeply for my mother. She was delighted to receive him in her nursing home, and he was delighted to be with her. It taught me a real lesson about forgiveness. I'm the kind of person who would never have forgiven him. But that doesn't really work if you want to have peace in your life.

About eight years ago, after my mother passed away, I tried to have it out with him to clear the air. I wasn't sure how much longer he'd be well enough to participate in a conversation like the one I wanted to have, and I had issues I wanted to resolve. What else to do with so many years of intense psychotherapy? So I dredged up my distant childhood memory of him taking me to see a woman when I was a child. He looked stricken, and stammered an apology. "I just wanted her to see how beautiful my daughter was," he said. Then I dredged up the old South Carolina abandonment story, which I had turned into a full-time obsession.

"I was just a little child, Dad. Do you have any idea of the effect that had on me?"

He looked confused and said it was so long ago he was surprised I had any memory of it at all. "And all I can say is that it was necessary so that we could put some money away before bringing you back to give you a better life," he said.

"And when you remarried and moved, Dad, you didn't give me your phone number and address. That brought up more abandonment issues for me." Am I a pain in the ass or what?

He denied he'd ever intended to disappear at all. It occurred to me that he might be telling the truth. But I could also see that he wasn't going to let me drag him into my psychodrama. He was an old man interested in peace in his family and he was due to go visit my mother, and so he ended our conversation by standing up and reaching out to give me a big hug. I still remember his arms around me in my sunny living room that looked out onto the city. He loved my new condo, he kept telling me that, and he was very pleased I had made the decision to downsize and prepare properly for my senior years.

"I'm very proud of you, you know that," he said. "And I love you very much."

And I don't know why, but that's all I really needed to hear. I think by then I was ready to let go of my heavy baggage, which was the weight of two Louis Vuitton trunks.

I still remember his last visit to my home. He had asked if he could come stay with me for the holidays. "But, Dad, Suzanne is planning to be in labor and I've got to be with her," I said. He told me he understood, and that he'd make other plans. But I didn't feel right about it. He had had a rough year, in and out of hospitals, and clearly wanted to come see his children. I didn't know if he'd be up for the trip another time. So I made the decision that he needed me more than Suzanne did. Her mother-in-law would be with her, a wonderful woman who raised three children. So my father came to me.

Suzanne's labor over the holidays, it turned out, was difficult. I kept calling and leaving messages in hope of hearing a report on how it was going, and I was hearing very little.

"Why don't you return my calls?" I finally stammered into her voice mail.

Eventually, she called back and said, "Why don't you stop these hysterical phone calls? You're just acting out because you're guilty that you're not here with me."

I stammered that it was more complicated than that. If I'd gone overseas, then my father, her grandfather, would not have been able to visit me in California for the holidays. "A new life is starting for you, but his is coming to a close, and he misses me," I told her.

Suzanne understood, of course. She was not interested in dwelling in resentment. And my father and I had a lovely visit. I loved watching how carefully he ate his healthy breakfasts, and I admired his self-discipline. He was a believer in healthy eating long before it had become fashionable. He had purchased a juicer for my apartment so he could use it on his visits. Juicing was something he believed in deeply, and he would make us delicious drinks from apples and carrots and celery and then explain their benefits. It was from him that I learned to eat more conscientiously. And when I realized how carefully he dressed each morning, I laughed out loud, and understood even better why it is that I am completely unable to just throw something on from my closet and leave my home in five minutes to run even the smallest of errands. I really am my father's daughter. We had such a nice visit, and there was real peace between us.

The only thing that was difficult was my sister. Lydia, who is fourteen years younger than me, has been unwell for years. It's not something I want to write about, but I think I've learned a few things about her situation that are worth sharing.

When my mother was alive, she refused to take her younger daughter's problems all that seriously because she was afraid, unsure of what to do. And for years, my father had a hard time facing facts about her, too.

It took me a long time to come to terms with the fact that there was little I could do to fix her. I should have seen the signs a lot earlier—she needed professional help. Fifty years ago, my mother used to be amazed because she would run off down the sidewalk without looking back with the normal fear of a little child. She was lively and mischievous, and my friends and I adored her. We were young teens who loved the idea of dressing up a pretty little baby and taking her out for a stroll. Just the sight of her tiny face waiting for me in the window of our brownstone in Harlem filled me with happiness when I'd come home from school. Often she would be singing as I walked through the door.

As a child, Lydia always had the capacity to make us all very happy. But as an adult, she became too much for any of us to understand, with incidents of behavior far beyond the understanding of anyone except professionals. Finally, after years of struggle to help her normalize her life, one of her doctors explained to me, "You have no power over any of this, and I've watched this kind of situation take over the lives of families over and over again."

"Yes, I know," I said. "She really has affected all our lives."

"Well, my suggestion is you make a deal with her," he continued. "Tell her that you will stand behind her one hundred percent if she will agree to get treatment. If she won't agree to that, she will never have a life and neither will you."

It was common sense, but until that moment I had never thought of it.

I told Lydia what this doctor said. She said she didn't need help. Days later, there was another terrible incident that upset our entire family. And it was around that time that I made a big decision. I looked at myself in the mirror, and I said, "You can't do this anymore, Diahann." So I called Lydia and told her, "I don't want to talk to you anymore unless it's about getting treatment. If you do that, I will pay for it, and continue to be around for you, and I will be there to help you start a new life the day of your release. If not, I'm finished, Lydia, we're through."

She didn't believe me. And frankly, I didn't believe myself, either.

But I have stuck to my word. Now we speak only a few times a year. But there isn't a day I don't hope to get a call saying that she has agreed to get help. As soon as that happens, I will get behind her 100 percent. Meanwhile, I lament the loss of our relationship. And I pray she will get well someday. But I don't drive myself wild with worry anymore. I have finally figured out that there are some things in life you can't control, and that there are some people you can't help until they are ready to be helped. Maybe I haven't done all I can. Maybe I have. But I now accept that my sister's problems may never be resolved. And as unsatisfying as it is, that's a resolution of sorts.

A few years ago, I drove past the old family brownstone in Harlem, and saw the front window in our parlor, and remembered little Lydia's face there, clear as sunlight.

My father had invited me to join him back at his beloved Abyssinian Baptist Church in Harlem. He was being honored for his years of service as a deacon. You can imagine how much pleasure it gave him to be back there with me. When I got there, I remembered walking up the stairs as a young girl in my little organza dresses and with bows in my hair. I remembered sitting in the beautiful pews under balconies flooded with light. I remembered being among such hopeful people, the hats, the gloves, my father so handsome in his black suit and tie. I remembered the inspirational sermons, the invigorating oratory, and, of course, singing in the choir. Most of all I remembered holding the hands of my parents. And I think I cried.

I always felt at home in that beautiful church, and I always felt so safe. This hardworking father of mine always made sure I was safe. He wanted to protect me so much that he once literally lifted a flirting stranger into the air and carried him down the block just to keep him away from me. (I was nine months pregnant at the time.) My father worried about every friend and boyfriend I had, every schooling and career decision I ever made. Maybe his choices weren't the most sophisticated. But his behavior always came from love. He worked to build an incredible life for me.

And now here I was with him at his old church to see him honored. I was delighted to meet the Reverend Calvin Butts, the pastor and a brilliant political figure in the community. I was thrilled to meet the children of children I remembered from sixty years ago. The level of discourse and community ideals in the sermon made me proud to be among this congregation. Later, my father introduced me to everyone and I cheerfully shook hands with great pride. He was ecstatic to see me enjoying our visit. And I was happy that he wanted to share this part of his life.

He was proud of me and I was proud of him.

He was financially independent. He'd really thought through his retirement years, and made some very good decisions about moving to a rest home and living near his family. I missed not having him closer, but he was loved and well cared for on his native East Coast, among friends and a church community he loved. And his sister, Eleanor, was just wonderful to him. I had been estranged from her for years, I don't even know why, frankly. But I made a point of telling her how grateful I was that she'd encouraged him to share her family. I told her what a comfort it was to know his sister was watching over him so lovingly.

Not long ago, a time came when I knew I had to see him. He was ninety-six and the cancer was finally taking its toll. The happy look on his face when I walked into his room was enough to stop my heart. "Would you look who's here," he said. "It's my daughter all the way from California!" He was weak, certainly, and he needed help feeding himself. But even when his sister and I and others were meeting with hospice workers about his end-of-life care, he was present, and alert. He remembered dates and business details from years ago, when asked for them. And I could tell he was at peace with where he was in his life, satisfied with what he had accomplished. There was only the faintest look of confusion on his face that I observed as my visit went on in those last days, as if he wanted to know what was wrong with him and what was going on exactly. He could get a little foggy from the medication in the pain patch he was wearing for the cancer, and a little anxious, even as the nurses fussed over him with what seemed to be genuine affection.

He really had seduced each and every one of them. And I just had to laugh. "Oh, Dad," I thought to myself as they hovered over him, "you really are incorrigible!"

The last time I saw my father he was being lifted in his wheelchair into a van. He was wearing a silly little cap that someone had bought him for the rough New Jersey winter weather, and there was a wistful look on his face as we said good-bye.

"So long, Dad," I said. "I'll see you soon."

He thanked me for coming. But he didn't say he'd see me soon.

I think he knew it was our last good-bye.

His funeral came just a couple weeks later, and I flew back to New Jersey to a service that his sister and I, other members of the family, and his church had helped to arrange. It took place in a part of the state that was lovely and as rural as my father's childhood landscape in South Carolina. The minister of the church, Father Saunders, presented me with a letter for the family from the Reverend Calvin Butts, and a resolution from his esteemed Abyssinian Baptist Church. It said: *Deacon Johnson was a mild-mannered, soft-spoken, well-dressed gentleman at all times. You could always depend on him to complete an assignment. He had a keen insight in the correct solutions of many common problems that we encounter every day. He seldom volunteered his thinking or problem solving. However, if asked, he would invariably come up with the best solution.*

That was my dad, a role model of clear thinking and restraint.

When the casket was brought in, it was covered with a simple cloth. I was sitting in the second row and I kept thinking, "My father is in that box." There in that box was the man who, when I was a child, had been so tall and strong that he could lift me up as if I were as light as a feather. There was the man who looked so dashing in my youth, when he'd be behind the wheels of his brand-new Chryslers. He was a man everyone thought of as austere. But I was always able to break through his stern demeanor and find a man full of warmth and love, imperfect as a father, perhaps, but still wonderful in the enormity of his caring.

The memorial service would have greatly pleased him. It had a simple elegance and dignity. I know my father would have

appreciated the decorum. I gave a short speech thanking everyone for attending, especially the deacons from the Abyssinian
Baptist Church, and how wonderful it was to know he'd been
loved by so many people in the communities where he'd chosen
to live. I didn't say it, but I was very happy to see that this
church—the community of which he had become a part of in
the last years of his life—was also an integrated one. It was another stretch, I thought, a leap of faith, really, for the racially
untrusting young man from Aiken, South Carolina. He had
lived the life he had chosen for himself, and cherished his multi-
racial grandchildren and great-grandchildren. He had lived to
experience this monumental shift in the world, which included
the first time a black man ran for president of the United
States.

The ride away from the funeral with my relatives was not
solemn. We spoke of him warmly, happy he had had such a
good, long, and, for the most part, healthy life.

He had been a wonderful influence on me—except I have
to admit that when I was flying home from the funeral with my
oldest family friend, Sylvia, I did something I never do: I asked
for a double portion of my meal, plus a glass of red wine, which
I never do, because the wine on airlines is quite undrinkable. I
realized that I was toasting my father, who only drank twice a
year, either a glass of Mogen David or Manischewitz. Sylvia
thought it was because I was trying to fill a void that had just
opened in my life—suddenly I had no parents. It's a strange
feeling no matter when it happens to you in your life, and one
that throws you for a while. But I wonder if my overeating
wasn't just a little bit of a momentary rebellion, too. My father,

after all, always ate so carefully. With him gone, and just hours after his funeral, I could finally make a complete and total glutton of myself.

When I arrived home, I was so bemused. I thought, "Dad, don't worry, that will never happen again," and I ate nothing the next day to make it up to him and to myself. And just a few days after his passing, I started using his juicer.

What a lucky woman I was to have had such good parents for so long.

And I'm so glad my father and I had a chance to reconcile, and have a proper and quiet good-bye just days before his passing. The peace we found with each other before it was too late is something that has brought great comfort to me. When you're forgiven, it makes you understand just how much you are loved. And when you forgive? The whole world opens up to you and you make yourself available to the highest form of happiness.

TEN

Brand-New Game

IT WAS A FRIDAY NIGHT IN APRIL OF 2006, IN NEW
York City, at Feinstein's at the Regency, and I was about to go on
with my brand-new one-woman show. I was standing in an
area far too tiny to be called backstage. It was a nook, really, a
holding area that was barely large enough to contain me and
my outsize worries. Through the pounding of my anxious heart,
I heard a full house out there, and they sounded happy. I was
not used to the sound of such an intimate full house; it's very
different from the sound of hundreds in a cavernous Vegas
room. Feinstein's cabaret space, which is perhaps the most prestigious in the whole country, only seats around a hundred people. They would be so close, I thought, that they'd be able to see
every line on my face and hear every quirk and quaver in my
delivery. Everything about me was completely accustomed to
having distance—a lot of room for grand illusions and
make-believe. You can't do that with an audience sitting under
you, looking at your shoes. I still remember during the earliest

days of my career, which was the last time I sang in a tiny space, a man actually told me that I was wearing cheap shoes. Maybe that was what started me on the road to bigger and bigger shows.

Now here I was, back to a level of intimacy that would allow me to actually see reactions on the faces in my audience. But I didn't want to see the face of the *New York Times* critic likely to skewer me.

The venue wasn't the only thing that was intimate. The material was, too. That was new to a lady who always felt that performers who talked too much about themselves were inappropriate bordering on vulgar. The most intimidating part of all for me was the size of the orchestra—not even an orchestra, a combo really, a septet. I had never performed with fewer than fourteen musicians. My delivery had always been about the big voice and big sound that came with big brass and string sections. How did I get myself into this?

I wasn't about small. I was always about big.

Remember, I grew up on MGM musicals that were as much about spectacle as melody. I learned the ropes on the stages of Catskills resorts, where everything from your dress to your gestures had to be as big as your voice. The clubs I played in New York had room for good-size orchestras. And from there, things got even bigger in Miami, Chicago, Tahoe, Reno, and Vegas. And let me tell you something, when you get used to having a twenty-five-piece orchestra and the range of power that all those musicians can muster without so much as a synthesizer or electric guitar, you feel that that's the sound you have to have when you perform—big, fluid, and elegant. You get used to it fast.

I mean, once you've sung a Kurt Weill medley with dozens of strings backing you up, it becomes impossible to imagine it any other way. My whole career became one in which I traveled "fully contained," as the term went, with musicians and staff. The gowns I wore and the numbers I picked were chosen as a way to dazzle audiences. From my earliest days, my shows seduced with their size, whether in Havana, where I performed in the late fifties for a society still holding on to its taste for the lavish, or in Paris, where I once performed at the Olympia, which is the Parisian Radio City Music Hall. I will never forget the night the orchestra got lost at that performance. The whole illusion of seamless spectacle was falling apart in front of an impeccably dressed French audience so enthralled with the glamour of an American Negro star. So I did something I had never done before. I stopped the orchestra and sang the rest of the song a capella. It was a very strange feeling, to be singing alone into the glaring lights of that enormous theater. And I thought it would be a total disaster. But the next day, I opened the papers to find that the critics loved it. Perhaps my voice and presence were enough to carry off a simpler kind of act. I paid no attention.

For years, my excessive level of production seemed anything but absurd to me. It's what audiences wanted in those big rooms, not just in Vegas, but all over the country. There was no questioning the cost. The size of the audiences would pay for it all.

And oh, did I love working with some of the most talented musicians and musical directors of their time. There is a melding that happens when you sing with a big orchestra, and you tend to become an instrument with them to create great sound-scapes in beautifully lit rooms with the perfect acoustics to belt and sashay and shimmer.

And television? It may be an intimate medium. But from the very beginning, its aim was to overwhelm. I would show up to be a guest star on *Carol Burnett* at this studio or that one around Hollywood through the 1960s and 1970s, and I'd find entire cities moving around. There were spectacular sets just to back up a song like "I Got Plenty of Nothing" or "The Best Things in Life Are Free." There would be armies of people employed, too. I was much too busy learning my steps and figuring out my wardrobe changes to think about it. And I have to say that I never took any of the glamour of it for granted. I'd find myself thinking, "Here I am on this show or this stage, me, this little girl from Harlem, and all these people are here working so I can sing."

Of course there were times when even I had to question the level of spectacle. When I had my summer variety series in the mid-1970s, we did a number, "I'll Go My Way by Myself." It was all about facing the world on my own. "No one knows better than I, myself, I'm by myself," I sang. And as I did, the clever director had all these people coming and going around me on the set, one to brush out and spray my hair, another to do my makeup, another to light me, another with a script to go over lines, until my little meditative song of solitude had turned into the three-ring circus I knew so well. That's what it was almost always like whenever I'd open my little mouth to sing. Big.

I still remember being in a number on *The Ed Sullivan Show* in his theater in New York. The song I was singing was

"Hum Drum Blues" by Oscar Brown. It was a gritty song about what it's like to be unable to escape the cycle of poverty, a political song for the moment, really, that reflected both the restlessness of the black community and the national fight for equality. We were rehearsing it, with its driving, urgent beat and urgent lyrics, and meanwhile there were all these dancers around me sashaying around with pink and yellow umbrellas. So I finally said, "Hold it, just a moment, please. Why are all these dancers around me with pink and yellow umbrellas?"

At the time, the show was being produced by Ed Sullivan's son-in-law. So he came out and asked, "What's the matter, Diahann?" I told him that the lyrics I had been singing were "Stuck in a rut going nowhere," and the name of the song was "Hum Drum Blues." I said that the song was about poverty and the ghetto and that twirling colorful umbrellas really made no sense. Now, I was still young at that time, and most assuredly I was not invited to have an opinion about such a gargantuan production number on such a gargantuan TV show. So my little question caused a big fuss. First the choreographer came out (I think it was Peter Gennaro) to deal with my question. Then my manager, Roy, and then half a dozen people were on that stage, all very agitated. Finally Ed Sullivan himself came onstage. He asked me what the trouble was.

"I'm singing about something I think is politically important," I told him. "And I don't understand all the pink and yellow umbrellas. I just don't get it."

And then Ed Sullivan, bless him, looked at the director and choreographer and the rest of this squad of creative individuals, all invested in creating the biggest spectacle they could, and he asked, "So what *do* the pink and yellow umbrellas represent?"

Nobody had a good answer. So they toned it down. It was one of the first times in my career that I understood that bigger was not necessarily better.

Bigger could actually be nothing.

Another time I had to question spectacle was when I starred in a television special with Maurice Chevalier. Ours was the first collaboration between French and American television, and we were to sing songs about Broadway and Paris, a real hands-across-the-water effort. I looked au courant in my tasteful, slightly mod outfits and bobbed hair, and Maurice Chevalier—well, who wouldn't adore the old man as he crooned?

The only trouble was the director.

He was some kind of avant-garde sensation and his goal was to create an Op-Art spectacle with his two stars and chorus. That's how we ended up with Monsieur Chevalier singing "Life Is Just a Bowl of Cherries" while, for reasons I will never understand, dancers in leotards moved around him holding up giant lips and mustaches. I don't remember anything I sang other than "I Love Paris." But I do remember trying to get through a song set against a set that was a maze of mirrors, and having to stop at the end of every phrase. You can't deliver any meaning to an audience if you can't sing a song through to the end. This was supposed to be art. Instead, it was boring, pretentious, and big in every way except emotionally. At the end of each day of shooting, France's most charming crooner and America's darling new singing sensation left feeling uninspired.

"Have a good evening, Monsieur Chevalier," I said.

"And the same to you," he'd reply.

Was I making the same mistake a few years later, with my act and its set—a towering construction made of Lucite? It looked dazzling on the Las Vegas stage on which I sang a song by a popular folksinger of the moment, Don McLean. The song was "Starry, Starry Night." It was about Vincent van Gogh. So why not project his famous stars all over the set at ten times the size they actually were in the painting? Never mind that the song was a delicate wisp of a ballad about suicide and sadness. We had rear-projection lighting that, in tandem with my orchestra, gown, and, oh yes, my lovely voice, would thrill even the most bored audience.

I had to do whatever I could to make an impact. By the 1970s, things had changed so much in my business that I was running in circles to keep up. Not only did I have to understand what Motown was about, I had to incorporate what Dionne Warwick was doing with Burt Bacharach's songs. I'd buy albums and cassettes in stores (and, soon enough, CDs) and listen to hundreds of songs on my living-room floor, in search of the new material that would help get me up-to-date. I found it exhausting. I also found the idea of replacing strings with synthesizers (not just for economic reasons, but to have a more contemporary sound) loathsome. Still, I kept my big act going, like the Big Top, with my full squad of staff and musicians at my side. I could not give up big.

Monte had told me years before that I should not be afraid of singing alone with a pianist, that I had the right voice and interpretive skills to pull off subtle and intimate. I didn't listen. I didn't have to. Eventually, though, things really started to dry up. The audiences in Vegas had changed. I remember doing one show in the early 1980s in Reno, in which I had to share the stage with an elephant.

She was really the star, not me. Talk about the elephant in the room.

I was being told to downsize everything—my act and my life—and I was ignoring it. Well, I managed to downsize my life sooner than my act. I got rid of the huge house, waterfall and billiards room included, and moved to a smaller house. Then, ten years later, when I started wondering who all these people were who were working at my smaller house—gardeners, housekeepers, cooks, and more—I decided to stop trying to pretend I was a billionaire and move to a condo. I even organized a sale to sell everything, and jumped in my car just as the first buyers were driving up. They bought things I never really needed in the first place. I couldn't get over it. I was gleeful at the idea of sending all my stuff out into the world.

It didn't take long to understand that living in a condo and driving a sedan rather than a Rolls was liberating. Yes, some privacy is compromised in a high-rise. But maybe all that privacy, all that exclusivity, is just a little overrated. It's nice to be greeted by neighbors in the lobby on a daily basis. It's nice to have a home and a staff that doesn't make you feel like you're hemorrhaging every hard-earned penny. I was downsizing and I was growing up! I didn't need all the accoutrements to show myself that I had a luxurious life.

Still, when Michael Feinstein first invited me to perform in his small cabaret space, I turned him down cold. "I wouldn't know what to do, Michael," I said.

"What do you mean, Diahann?" he asked.

"What am I going to do without my orchestra?"

"How many do you work with?"

"Twelve is usually the minimum."

"Four would work better in such a small space."

"That's why you don't want me, Michael. I can't be at my best if I can't take all my stuff with me."

"Well, won't you think about it?"

I've always liked Michael. He isn't just a wonderful pianist, singer, and impresario. He's a wonderful man. I trust him. Several months later, an offer came in from him through my manager. Would I please do a show at his space at the Regency? That's when I seriously started to think about what it would be like to put an act together for a small room. There have been some wonderful one-woman shows in recent years and I thought perhaps I could find my way to creating my own. So I finally found myself warming to the idea and saying to my agent, "Well, let's try. Let's see what we can do."

First, we made calls to see who was still around to work with. I needed a director, for starters. And when I was able to reach Larry Grossman after many calls, I said to him, "Thank God you're alive!" We found Lee Norris, my old musical director of twenty years, too . . . hallelujah. And little by little we got this minuscule group together and started working.

And that's how I began the process of walking myself into the twenty-first century.

This showbiz dinosaur was going to evolve!

I was not expecting much when Lee, my musical director, suggested I come to New York to hear the band he'd pulled together. After all, it was only seven pieces. With my history of fronting orchestras of ninety musicians, and my regular routine of performing with a twenty-eight-piece group, fourteen at the smallest, what would this minuscule septet have to offer? Everything, it turned out. I could not believe how good the group sounded. They were top-level East Coast musicians, raised on Broadway and working around the greats, and what they sounded like was so inspiring I felt I needed a well-written show to rise to the occasion. Choosing songs was familiar. I've done that all my life. But what the hell was I going to *say* to this audience looking right up my nose?

My shows had never been intimate. Just the opposite, actually. Now I had to come up with a script that was conversational, confessional, and entertaining. Larry found a talented writer, Stuart Ross, the creator of the hit show *Forever Plaid*. But when I sat down with him for the first time, things didn't click. It took time and patience to find each other. Then he had an idea.

"Why don't we look you up on eBay?" he asked.

So we went onto my computer, and with his touch of a button, my life flashed before my eyes. Posters from movies. Issues of magazines with me on the cover, including *Good Housekeeping,* which made me laugh because I never was and never will be a domestic goddess. Vinyl albums. A canceled check from Samuel Goldwyn. A tabloid headline that said DIAHANN WARNS DORIS DAY THAT NO MAN IS WORTH CRAWLING AFTER NO MATTER HOW LONELY IT GETS. Another old tabloid with a cover suggesting that Vic had Mafia ties and, by marriage, so did I. Julia lunch boxes, paper dolls, and Barbies. DVDs of me on *Sonny and Cher* and *The Flip Wilson Show*. Photos of me and Joan Collins on *Dynasty* with those big-shouldered Nolan Miller gowns.

A landfill of detritus! My life had been reduced to this?

Not at all, Stuart assured me. But it was a start for putting together a show.

He got me to tell stories, the kind I'd never told before. Such as the time when my love life was at its lowest, and I booked a suite at the Plaza with the intention of doing myself in. First, I got my hair styled and trotted over to Bergdorf's to buy a stunning nightgown with matching lace-and-satin peignoir. When I got to the hotel (with three sleeping pills and a bottle of Cristal in my Louis Vuitton overnight case), I was informed that a mistake had been made and I could not have the suite until the following day. I was offered a room instead by the service elevator. A room by the service elevator? I wouldn't be caught dead (literally) in anything less than a suite! I was frantic. In my typically controlling way, I had it all planned and now it was falling apart. So I called a friend. She rushed over and we had dinner and polished off the champagne and ended up laughing until dawn. And the next day, I put my whole life back together.

Stuart was also tickled when I told him that I'd been proposed to twice at the Regency, where my show would be playing. Here's what we came up with: "I had two previous engagements here, one on the third floor, one on the eleventh. So when I was asked to consider this engagement tonight, my first impulse was to ask, 'How many carats?'"

We Googled. We giggled. We went riffling through my

life. And as we did, something very interesting began happening over and over again. I found that despite my tendency in the
past to take every single thing so seriously, and to consider myself something of a victim as I inspected every crevice of my
psyche, I was laughing.

And I was overjoyed when Bob Mackie made me the sweet-
est little dress for my return to the New York stage. I told him I
wanted something understated. For once in my life, I didn't
want to hear people talking about my dress after a show as if
it were the star, not me. Plus, he needed to come up with something modest in size, a dress that would not take up an entire
room. That way, I would not ruin people's hairdos as I threaded
my way past them through the back of the little cabaret space to
get onto the stamp-size stage. The dress Bob made was diminu-
tive in size and demure in look, like a schoolgirl dress—black
and white with a Peter Pan collar. And, oh yes, there were also
thousands of tiny little glittering beads that sparkled like the
skyline. The dress cost thirteen thousand dollars. It went very
well with my "Give Me the Simple Life" medley, I have to say.

On opening night, nervous as I'd ever been, I stepped onto
that stage in front of my first New York audience in forty years.
And I looked straight down onto the smiling face of none other
than my friend Harry Belafonte. I could hear people breathing
in that small room. Their proximity was indeed unsettling. But
the band sounded great and I sang well, and when I told my first
joke and heard the laughter, it was better than anything I'd
heard in years. Frightened as I was to talk about my life, my
loves, my ups and downs, it turned out that being honest and
intimate, admitting to the big regrets and owning up to my

funny foibles, forced me to face myself as a performer in ways I'd never tried before.

And I am not being disingenuous when I tell you that I was shocked by the generosity of the *New York Times* review. Not only was my singing described as "erupting as if from a volcano." I was called "an astonishingly youthful" seventy-year-old grandmother. Fortunately it was only the *show* that was referred to as "historic," and not me. But actually, let's face it—I am historic. There is hardly a place I haven't been that doesn't have history for me. And everywhere I travel, there is someone to see.

And this new solo show of mine, something I had resisted because I was always a lady who needed things big . . . well, it's turning into a big fat blessing for me. It's years after that *New York Times* review and presenters in venues from all over the country still call and invite me to come tell my stories, sing a song, do my thing. How can I say no?

Last November, Michael Feinstein invited me to be part of a show at a large theater in the Palm Springs area. I was delighted. I spent the previous week rehearsing in Los Angeles, primping and preparing and getting everything just so in order to give a flawless performance. I needed to be in shape for the stage—in fighting form. The theater was a thousand-seat house— a good size for the old girl. And although it was supposed to be Michael's evening, he was gracious enough to offer to share equal billing with me. That's more than I can say for some men I've performed with in my lifetime!

On the afternoon of the show, I arrived and walked onstage to rehearse with the band and with Michael. That's when I felt

my throat going completely hoarse. That tickle I had been trying to brush off the day before was now manifesting itself as a
full-blown, song-eating sore throat, a showstopper—but not in
a good way.

My manager, Brian, didn't miss a beat and called a local
doctor. Then I excused myself from rehearsal with little
drama—as if I were just going to use the powder room—and I
was whisked out of that theater and into a nearby doctor's office, where I was rigged up to a machine that blew something
into my lungs . . . cortisone, I guess; don't ask me—I don't
even know how to send e-mails . . . and then whisked right
back. It was kind of dramatic, a performing-arts emergency.
But Brian had seen it all before. Peggy Lee, whom he had managed years ago, traveled with her own machinery for just such
emergencies. And the result was that her lungs were always
strong and her audiences always happy. That's what it is always,
always about for me and any performer worth her paycheck:
making an audience happy by doing what makes you happy.
It's the greatest luxury in the world to be able to call that
work.

Back at the theater (which, I was told, I had headlined
when it opened in 1986) I got on the stage with Michael. The
band started playing, and was sounding great. We rehearsed "I
Wish I Were in Love Again" and "Who's Sorry Now?" and a few
other feisty hits that make love sound more like war than romance. (Later in the evening, I dedicated them "to all my hus-
bands.") I went through each song with Michael as best I could.
But there was no doubt that my throat was not in any shape for
a good concert.

"Oh, Michael," I apologized. "I have a terrible frog in my throat."

"Well then, you might as well enjoy it," he replied.

And you know what? That's just what I did. Well, why not?

As I told the audience later, after Michael was kind enough to introduce me as "essential" to them, I thought I'd be dead by now. And besides, sore throat or not, I got to wear false eyelashes and a big blue gown to work—a getup that most women would be able to wear only on a red carpet or to a gala. Best of all, I was working with my friend and singing the songs I loved so dearly. I love working. It keeps me in touch with what makes me happy.

At my age, I revel in every performance even with a frog in the throat. It's surprising to find I can still be such a little trouper at seventy-two. But I'm not alone in this. Everywhere I go, I find women my age having a ball just rolling with the punches.

I mean, look at the change in the conversations we have these days about menopause. There are jokes about it on television, on talk shows and sitcoms and commercials. For women, it's wonderful to be out of the closet with this little affliction. It was actually a word nobody wanted to hear for years. Menopause meant that you were unattractive and that everything was on its last legs. So even the mention of the word would provoke people to say, "Oh, don't say that." But I just love the fact that we are owning our bodies now, and that you can be at dinner with a friend who starts fanning herself with her hand and she can just say, "Oh, give me a second, I'm having a senior moment!" We are free enough to fan our faces in solidarity and enjoy it. I love it! It isn't just good for senior women, it's good for all women. How far we've come! Jay Leno now makes jokes about women who have to wear little pads because their bladders aren't as strong as they used to be. Maybe it's a little more vulgar than is appropriate. But it's absolutely funny and true.

Not long ago, we shot the cover of this book. In my typical fashion, I had spent a great deal of time preparing for the shoot. Greg, my favorite photographer in the world, was on board. And a dozen designer dresses had been sent over from Saks. They all fit as if they'd been designed just for me. But guess what? When I tried them on again the day before the shoot, I realized they were too tight. I had blossomed a full size since I'd last checked. How did that happen? I'd been exercising. I'd been watching my diet. It might have been my estrogen having its way with my body—something women of my age rarely talk about. The breasts get bigger without your permission, and like everything else we have to face when we hit our senior years, it can be a real roller coaster. Or perhaps I should say a Thanksgiving Day parade. I felt as big on top as a balloon in every outfit I had specifically chosen for that shoot. I don't know why I hadn't been prepared. These days I always travel to my shows with gowns in several sizes. I never know what size will fit me and I don't want to take any chances. So in addition to all the other things I have to worry about when preparing to perform, it's imperative I provide myself with enough wardrobe options to deal with a body that seems to have a mind of its own.

I remember, several years ago, being in the dressing room of the couture floor of Saks in Beverly Hills, a place I always enjoy, and the salesgirl pulled clothes for me in what her records showed was my size, and what I thought was my size, too. So why was I having trouble with all the buttons and zippers?

"What's wrong?" I asked as I struggled.

That's when my girlfriend said very quietly, "They're too small, Diahann."

"What do you mean they're too small? Eight is my size."

"But they're too small, Diahann. Would you please give yourself a break and let her bring them in the next size or maybe even the next size after that?"

I told her I had been working like a dog to keep in shape. And I asked her what it was she was trying to tell me by suggesting I get things two sizes bigger.

"I'm telling you that your body has changed," she said.

"Not that much, it's not possible," I said.

"Yes." She sighed. "It changes that much. All the fat glands have changed and the weight is redistributed in your body, and it's not really within your control anymore, so you just have to go along with it."

I stood on that gorgeous couture floor at Saks with my thoughts running in every direction. Finally I asked, "Does this mean I won't be able to wear couture anymore?" The salesgirl looked down, then fled from the dressing room, as if from the scene of a crime. And my friend told me, "If you go up to a size fourteen, I think you're going to be in trouble with couture." What a dire possibility that was!

Well, I have not gone to a size fourteen. I am holding at twelve as best I can. But I suppose if I do get up to fourteen, I can always take my favorite gowns and have them copied. I do have my ways of making anything work when it comes to clothes.

So why had I let myself get into this position with the clothes for my photo shoot? My body was rebelling on me at the worst possible time.

I did what any self-respecting and terribly vain Beverly Hills lady would do in such an emergency. I bought an over-the-counter water pill and took it before going to bed the night before the shoot. Within an hour, I was sweating like a race-horse. The water pill was definitely working and the weight was coming off. I was up and down, in and out of bed, all night, sweating, bathing, then finding I could squeeze into outfits that would have nothing to do with me just hours before. I lost four pounds by dawn. But when I woke up later, all the weight was back—as if, in the words of the great Sir Andrew Lloyd Webber, we never said good-bye. I didn't find that out until I arrived at the shoot and could not fit into anything. My bosom was bust-ing out all over (as Oscar Hammerstein once wrote). What a disaster. Had it been any other time but now, my golden years, it would have been cause to stop the music and call everything off. But at this shoot, with all that camera equipment and all those people expecting me to shine, I found myself determined to make it work, just as I had a few months before when my throat deserted me in Palm Springs. Well, what are you going to do? You have to learn at my age that you can only fight your body and your metabolism so much. If you don't come to terms with that, what fun are you going to have on your last years on earth?

So you know what I did? I borrowed the shirt off my photographer's back. That's right. It was black, which is so much more slimming than the colors I had originally selected, and it fit me well enough to do its job. "This is fine," I said. "Let's get started." We tried various poses, and made sure to get my legs in the frame because, bless them, they're still slim. Greg worked his photographer's magic, moving me this way and that. And you know what? We had fun and we got our shot.

No, it isn't of a lady with a body to die for—all my Pilates training notwithstanding. The lady on the cover of this book is one who has lived and still has some lines of experience on her face—at least before the retoucher got to it. The lady on the cover may or may not be the perfect mother or grandmother, and heaven knows she has never been very good at selecting men. But you know what she most definitely is? She's happy. I hope you like her. I do. Some people come of age as teenagers. I came of age as a senior citizen. Now, if you'll excuse me, I have to get myself ready to go out to dinner. It will take a little time and effort. As I have said, I really don't know who I am until I've put on my makeup. And you know what? You wouldn't know me, either.

Acknowledgments

If the process of childbirth were anything like this book's unexpected five-year gestation, no one would ever choose to have children. So now we have this bouncing baby, not the product of my loins but rather of my angst. Since this book is about lessons learned, the journey was by definition rather painful. As a senior citizen, it's been a long road in any case, and I'm no doubt forgetting to thank all of the contributors to this delivery. For that, I'm deeply sorry.

First and foremost, I owe a special thanks to my editor, Dawn Davis, who went beyond the traditional editor's role with creative input, advice, perspective, and pep talks. Her vision and perseverance were absolutely material to whatever success this book enjoys. I can't believe she managed to have two beautiful children during this journey as well!

My coauthor, Bob Morris, did a superlative job weaving together my experiences into a cohesive narrative, which was anything but an easy task. I enjoyed our afternoons together as we plumbed the depths and revisited the heights of my life, thankful for his insightful writing style and editing skills.

I spent the initial part of this creative process with Robin Stone—because of family matters we were unable to continue. But I thank you, Robin, a lovely young woman.

Christina Morgan, Dawn's assistant, expended a great deal of effort doing photo research and licensing. She was ever pleasant on the phone and diligent in keeping the paperwork flowing.

My sincere thanks to the entire production department for their visual design, their superb copyediting, and for bending over backward to accommodate the impact of my work schedule on their deadlines.

Susan Fales-Hill, my niece, lovingly shared her experience with writing her own manuscript, and constantly reminded me whenever I was screaming and climbing the walls that it was all "part of the process."

We've all been able to count on Carol Mann, my literary agent, for seeing all sides of any issues, for her honesty and refreshing common sense. She's one of the finest human beings I've ever met.

My wholehearted gratitude goes to my manager, Brian Panella, for keeping me on track and focused, in all aspects of my life as well as on this book.

Jeffrey Lane, my publicist, I must thank for all his care in helping me to project the best of myself, and for his coordination with the HarperCollins public relations department; they worked beautifully together.

My heartfelt thanks to my daughter, Suzanne, for sharing

her thoughts and positive suggestions, as well as for holding my feet to the fire throughout the entire experience. Thank goodness we love and trust each other.

And to Lynne Glazer for helping me pull it all together toward the end—photo research and acquisition using "the machine," helping me edit and submit additional stories through several iterations of drafts through the bound galleys.

IRVING BERLIN

February 7th, 1968

Dear Diahann Carroll:

The way you sang those songs last night on
the Tonight Show made me feel awfully good.

With my thanks and best wishes, I am

Sincerely,

Irving Berlin

Miss Diahann Carroll
173 Riverside Drive
New York, N. Y.